I'm looking forward to reading this book. I hope it sheds light in some
murky corners.

Ken Loach
film director

As the global economy lurches from one catastrophe to the next, with the
ever widening gulf between the haves and have-nots and the paradigm
of economic expansion über alles bringing us to the brink of ecological
crisis, *A House of Cards* provides a lucid and accessible introduction to the
concepts and contradictions underpinning the system, and outlines the
changes that need to happen for a more sustainable and equitable future.

Kevin Smith
author of *The Carbon Neutral Myth*

A House of Cards

from fantasy finance to global crash

Action Guide No. 2

Gerry Gold & Paul Feldman

Published by Lupus Books
PO Box 942
London SW1V 2AR

www.aworldtowin.net
info@aworldtowin.net

ISBN 978-0-9523454-3-5

A House of Cards illustration by Ellen Graubart
Cover design Nick Feldman
Design and typography by Robbie Griffiths
Printed and bound by CPI Antony Rowe Ltd
Chippenham Wiltshire SN14 6LH

Contents

Contents

Introduction

A House of Cards is nothing if not timely. As the global financial and economic crisis deepens, politically active people tell us that the world of derivatives, hedge funds, private equity and wholesale money markets is beyond their understanding. So *A House of Cards* sets out to demystify the financial system and show its inescapable relationship to productive activity. The authors explain the way in which the component parts of the global economy interact and drive each other.

In particular, *A House of Cards* shows how the contradiction between productive capital and what Marx called "fictitious capital" – the world of fantasy finance – is driving the global economy into slump. We also spell out the consequences of corporate-driven globalisation, including climate change and growing inequality. There is a response to those who argue that the solution lies – impossibly – in better regulation of global capital before the authors set out a detailed vision of a future economy based on co-ownership, self-management and sustainability.

As *A House of Cards* goes to print, the debt contagion is spreading fast. On 30 October, UBS – Europe's largest bank – announced that it had written off $5.6 billion in sub-prime and other bad loans in the third quarter. Pre-tax profit forecasts were abandoned in favour of substantial losses. UBS had already sacked 1,500 staff including its head of investment. The bank's new chief executive Marcel Rohner admitted that "current difficulties" would not be "be resolved in the short term".

The same day, Merrill Lynch boss Stan O'Neal jumped before he was pushed following the investment bank's heavy sub-prime losses. O'Neal lost the confidence of the board after the bank ran up liabilities of $4 billion.

Also on 30 October, the gathering recession in the US economy saw consumer confidence slump to a two-year low, while house prices in August suffered their biggest fall in 16 years. The devaluation of the dollar gathered pace. The next day brought no better news. It emerged that Northern Rock had borrowed over £22 billion in government-backed loans from the Bank of England, leaving each UK taxpayer poorer to the tune of £730. The failing mortgage lender is expected to need £40 billion to shore it up, transferring the equivalent of half the annual budget for the NHS into the private sector.

Then on 4 November, Citigroup – the world's largest bank – shocked the financial world by parting company with Chuck Prince, its chief executive and chairman, after acknowledging sub-prime market losses of up to $11 billion. The bank was left holding "collateralised debt obligations" not worth the paper they are printed on because the market for selling them on no longer exists. Citigroup built its "assets" – primarily its lending – by an astonishing 48% in 21 months and the bank's sub-prime crisis is only the tip of its debt iceberg.

The social and political impact of the deepening crisis is certain to be profound, especially in Britain. Here, economic growth was largely founded on a consumption boom financed by house price inflation and easy credit. First the Tories and then New Labour encouraged this as part of the deregulation/globalisation process. These special conditions helped create an alienated sense of rampant individualism and a me-first outlook which has tended to overwhelm traditions of collective thinking and action. Those excluded from this instant "wealth" have too often become victims of the globalised drugs market as well as punitive penal policies.

Now millions of people are drowning in debt and the days of free-for-all consumption are coming to an end. For the majority, it was an illusion of wealth, a fantasy spun by credit card companies, corporations, advertising and marketing gurus and politicians from Thatcher to Blair and Brown. As reality reasserts itself, the conditions for revolutionary social change will also reappear. *A House of Cards* is above all a contribution by A World to Win towards building a movement that can achieve a sustainable economic and social system in place of the disastrous and ruinous market economy.

Paul Feldman
Editor, November 2007

1

Corporate power out of control

August, even though it is in the middle of the holiday season, is a month when great historic moments often take place. While they might seem to come out of the blue, these momentous events are, of course, the product of deeper conflicts and processes.

In August 1914, the First World War began when years of inter-imperialist rivalry exploded in military conflict. On 15 August 1971, the American government finally terminated the Bretton Woods financial system that had underpinned the post-1945 economic boom. In August 1991, a group of hard-line Stalinists attempted a coup in Moscow that precipitated the collapse of the Soviet Union later that year.

Then on 9 August 2007, the long period of corporate-driven globalisation of the world economy came to an abrupt end. That Thursday, major banks suddenly refused to lend to each other and a "credit crunch" hardened the arteries of the global financial system.

Behind the bankers' mutual fear was the unknown – how much bad debt did each hold as a result of the collapse of the so-called sub-prime housing market in the United States? But why were major banks even concerned about the failure of low-income American households to make their mortgage payments? For an explanation, we turn to *The Economist*, the business journal of free-market capitalism. The magazine has celebrated globalisation as a new "paradigm" of permanent growth and low inflation which benefits everyone from shareholders to cleaners.

In a special report on the world economy and the credit crunch, *The Economist* explained:

> A brilliantly inventive generation has harnessed computing power and financial theory to transform the world of finance. Trillion-dollar global markets have sprung up on the back of techniques for converting loans, interest payments, default risk and who knows what else into new securities that could be chopped up and repackaged in mind boggling combinations, sold and resold. (20 October 2007)

A by-product was credit for all, even those without any income! By 2006, a fifth of all new mortgages in America were to sub-prime borrowers which included people on welfare benefits. They were lured by low introductory interest rates and rising housing prices. These had risen by 124% between 1997 and 2006 and would surely go on increasing ad infinitum. Or so it seemed. In 2006, house prices began to fall and higher interest rates led to large-scale defaults and repossessions. Let *The Economist* take up the story:

> Meanwhile, financial assets of all sorts, from credit-card receivables to companies' debt repayments, had been turned into securities that could be bought and sold. Mortgages – both sub-prime and mainstream – were no exception. Lenders no longer needed to keep loans on their books, but could sell bundles of them to banks and investment funds at home or abroad. Properly designed, these complicated instruments could be stamped 'AAA' by helpful rating agencies. And, like any other security, they could be used as collateral by their lenders. By divorcing lenders from the risk of default, securitisation reduced their incentives to look carefully at their borrowers... And no one, least of all financial regulators, could be quite sure who in the global financial system was on the hook for which risks.

As the sub-prime crisis began to bite, American investment banks declared hundreds of billions of dollars of bad debt. Then banks in France and Germany revealed that they were involved too. And on that Thursday in August, the crisis went global. Overnight interbank rates in the euro zone shot up from 4% to 4.6% and the next day the European Central Bank astonished the financial world by injecting €95 billion into the money markets, closely followed by the Federal Reserve Bank in the US.

The origins of globalisation

But the sub-prime crisis is merely the sharpest expression to date of a global economy that is drowning in debt. These debt mountains have been built up over a 30-year period of globalisation and came into existence as a result of the needs of increasingly powerful corporations. At the heart of their dilemma was the fact that corporations could only expand on a global basis through the medium of credit while consumers could only purchase the vast numbers of commodities through borrowings of their own.

In little more than three decades, this process transformed a highly-regulated economy in which thousands of nationally-based companies were protected by governments into a globalised capitalist economy, in which a handful of transnational corporations (TNCs) exercise fantastic power and influence. No more than 100 TNCs dominate the global economy in all areas – from food to football, from oil to film and music, from banking to power generation.

Corporate requirements have come to determine the policies and actions of national governments and international agencies. Many

---

Key ingredients of capitalist globalisation

- ▶ trade and corporate deregulation
- ▶ the unrestricted movement of capital
- ▶ international, unregulated financial markets
- ▶ privatisation of public services
- ▶ commodification of new areas such as human DNA
- ▶ new forms of ownership such as intellectual property rights
- ▶ integration of national economies into a global system
- ▶ increased corporate concentration through global firms
- ▶ incorporation of new geographic areas into global production
- ▶ incorporation of new commodities into production – the commodification of everything
- ▶ erosion of traditional powers and policies of nation states
- ▶ global cultural homogenisation.

TNCs, like the food giant Wal-Mart, generate revenues larger than many national economies and international trade is formed largely of imports and exports within the corporations.

As they restlessly shift operations from place to place to rationalise production and drive down costs, the corporations have transformed South East Asia and China into world centres for production and India into a global service provider. The world's food is now controlled by a handful of agro-corporations, who determine prices and drive down quality through industrial methods of farming.

The TNCs' hunger for oil and other raw materials, and their need to expand markets into new regions, lies behind the wars in Iraq and Afghanistan, with all the human misery they have produced. A new period of forced extraction of minerals in Africa fuels countless civil wars. The unprecedented and reckless growth in output has driven the warming of the planet and accelerated climate change to danger point.

Corporate-driven globalisation has its origins in a period of slump and revolutionary struggles that marked the end of the 20-year boom that characterised the post-World War II period following the Bretton Woods agreement. This agreement was reached by 730 delegates from all 44 Allied nations who gathered at the Mount Washington Hotel in Bretton Woods, New Hampshire for the United Nations monetary and financial conference for three weeks in July 1944. They created a system of fixed currencies and tight controls on the movement of capital. Governments

Top 10 TNCs ($millions)

	Revenues	Profits
Wal-Mart	351,139	11,284
Exxon Mobil	347,254	39,500
Shell	318,845	25,442
BP	274,316	22,000
General Motors	207,349	-1,978
Toyota Motor	204,746	14,055
Chevron	200,567	17,138
DaimlerChrysler	190,191	4,048
ConocoPhillips	172,451	15,550
Total Oil	168,356	14,764

Source:: Forbes Global 500, February 2007

attempted to control their economies and currencies through monetary and fiscal policies. At the heart of the arrangement was a link between the dollar and gold at an exchange rate of $35 an ounce.

But capitalism's inbuilt drive to expand and grow made these restrictions unworkable and inflation and crisis replaced full employment. In the late 1960s, the capitalist system was shaken to its core as mounting opposition to the US war against the Vietnamese merged with a wave of militancy around the world, raising the possibility of revolutionary change. France was hit by a general strike and factory occupations in 1968 and the workers of Czechoslovakia defied a Soviet invasion aimed at crushing the democracy movement. Controlled money growth gave way to uncontrolled inflation. The Vietnam war was financed not by increased taxes but by printing more dollars. On 15 August 1971 the tension between the expanding volume of dollars and gold finally forced President Nixon to sever the relation between the two. The Americans had torn up Bretton Woods.

With the failure of mass struggles to challenge capitalism for power, governments around the world, led by the United States, jettisoned what was left of Bretton Woods in a bid to liberate the capitalist economy from its straitjacket. The regulations which had provided the basis for post-war reconstruction were terminated. National economies started to open up to foreign investment. The corporations underwent a rapid evolution, at each stage growing quickly, becoming more productive, and more destructive. They reached and breached limits by changing form to take on new characteristics. From their geographically-limited origins, nationally-rooted companies attained multinational status by exporting capital investment. They established copycat production plants in countries where they had or were developing markets to evade national trade barriers and import tariffs. They learned new accounting skills that enabled them to maximise profits by taking advantage of differing tax regimes in the countries in which they operated.

Historically, the capitalist state superstructure came into existence to preserve, sustain and develop the existing property relations. The state has evolved and changed in order to reflect new circumstances. The globalisation period proved no exception to this inter-related and reciprocal process. Key governments emerged to support these changes, led by Margaret Thatcher in Britain and Ronald Reagan in the USA. They oversaw a dramatic liberalisation of finance and trade regulations in their countries. This freeing up of financial markets was facilitated by and drove the advance of new communications technology.

This process was speeded up by the re-entry of the Soviet Union and Eastern Europe into the world capitalist markets. Global corporations and governments conspired through the IMF to ensure that there was not a regeneration of socialism in the Soviet Union, as Mikhail Gorbachev sought, but that the pro-capitalist forces triumphed under Boris Yeltsin.

Established in 1995, the WTO

▶ is a permanent institution based in Geneva with a 500-strong secretariat
▶ is the only international body whose authority the United States accepts
▶ opens markets for the benefit of transnational corporations
▶ administers dozens of international trade agreements and declarations
▶ handles and adjudicates on trade disputes
▶ monitors national trade policies
▶ has a legal personality and the power to enforce its rulings
▶ makes rulings which take precedence over agreements such as the Universal Declaration of Human Rights.

What the WTO controls

▶ General Agreement on Trade in Services, which deregulates public services
▶ Trade Related Intellectual Property Rights, which set enforceable global rules on patents, copyrights, and trademarks
▶ Trade Related Investment Measures, which dictate what governments can and cannot do in regulating foreign investment
▶ Agreement on the Application of Sanitary and Phytosanitary Standards, covering food safety, animal and plant health
▶ Financial Services Agreement, established to remove obstacles to the free movement of financial services corporations
▶ Agreement on Agriculture, setting rules on the international food trade
▶ Agreement on Subsidies and Countervailing Measures, which sets limits on what governments may and may not subsidise
▶ Agreement on Technical Barriers to Trade, set up to limit national regulations that interfere with trade.

The enforcers

Constraints on capital had to be removed globally, not just in a few countries. The collective interests of competing corporations found expression in global enforcers such as the World Trade Organisation, the International Monetary Fund, the World Bank and trading blocs like the European Union. These were able to wrest power away from national governments, to bring about a compulsory liberalisation of trade and financial markets and impose it on every country.

A new sort of corporation arose in the 1990s which sought to optimise the location of raw material sources, component production and final assembly in relation to availability of cheaper labour. Some of the more advanced corporations rationalised their operations on a global basis, using sophisticated management techniques to organise the production chain across continents.

100 corporations rule the world

In 2007, the top 100 corporations ranked according to revenues, amassed $10,228 billion in sales and made profits of $696 billion. Their total revenues were almost the same as the gross domestic product (GDP) of the United States – the world's largest economy - which in 2006 was estimated at $11,360 billion. The GDP of the major OECD economies – which still excludes India and China - in 2006 was $29,261 billion. So just 100 corporations generated nearly 35% of the total.

Wal-Mart was ranked number one in the Fortune 500 list of world corporations. The food retailer's revenues alone were $351 billion and its profits totalled $11.3 billion. Wal-Mart's revenues on their own were greater than many developed economies, including the GDPs of Greece, Austria, Belgium, and Turkey. In fact, Wal-Mart was the 13th largest "economy"! The corporation owns Asda in Britain and employs 1.9 million worldwide.

The top 10 corporations had total revenues of $2,435 billion – larger than each of the GDPs of Italy, France, Germany or the UK. The United Nations Commission on Trade and Development (UNCTAD) estimates that the world's largest 100 TNCs in 2004 accounted for 11%, 16% and 12% respectively of the estimated foreign assets, sales and employment of all TNCs operating throughout the world. Their total assets increased by 10% between 2003 and 2004. UNCTAD estimates that 65% of the affiliates of the world's largest TNCs are located in countries other than where the corporations have their headquarters.

The new type of corporation emerged through the door of foreign direct investment (FDI). FDI is where a company invests in developing industry in another country – for example the Japanese-owned Nissan plant in Sunderland. In 1980, the total of FDI exported by corporations globally came to just $54bn. By 1990, the total had leapt to $230bn. It soared to its peak in 2000, when $1,239bn – 23 times the level of 1980 – was invested in other countries. Following the global recession early in the new millennium, surging growth pushed China to invest abroad in its search for oil and raw materials. By 2006, FDI was back at $1,216bn, close to the peak.[1]

These new globalising corporations tend to employ few workers directly but set up sub-contracts with local producers who take on the role of employer. The top 100 TNCs work with an estimated 21,500 affiliates or local companies.

In little more than three decades, the ownership of capitalist companies has been transformed. From being largely owned by individuals and identified with the countries in which they originated, they have become a web of transnational and global corporations, linked by inter-corporate networks of ownership and interlocking directorates, transacting business through global financial markets. Many less agile companies have fallen prey to bigger predators keen to absorb the competition through waves of mergers and acquisitions.

Case study: General Motors

The world's largest maker of motor vehicles either owns, has or has had strategic alliances with the German Opel, British Vauxhall, Swedish Saab and as well as having complex and changing relationships with Italian Fiat, Australian Holden and South Korean Daewoo and Toyota, Suzuki and Isuzu of Japan. GM also has or has had advanced technology collaborations with DaimlerChrysler AG and BMW AG of Germany, Toyota Motor Corp. of Japan, and vehicle manufacturing ventures with several automakers around the world, including Shanghai Automotive Industry Corp. of China, AVTOVAZ of Russia and Renault SA of France. As early as 1972, GM was already operating in Chile, Malaysia, Iran, and the Philippines. As well as motor vehicles, GM has related interests in space travel and electronics and a finance company GMAC. GM has been struggling with rapidly changing conditions in the global economy in the 21st century, making a $10.6 billion loss in 2005 and losing its top slot to Toyota as measured by sales revenue in the first quarter of 2007. Its profits in the first quarter dropped 90%, heavily affected by losses from GMAC which had become caught up in the US housing market slump.

Profit, profit, profit

There is no secret to the motivation for the global corporations. In 1962, in *Capitalism and Freedom*, economist Milton Friedman set it out quite simply:

> There is one and only one social responsibility of business – to use its resources and engage in activities designed to increase its profits so long as it stays within the rules of the game, which is to say, engages in open and free competition without deception or fraud.

Here then is the driving force of the system which ensures that pharmaceutical corporations fight hard to prevent the production and distribution of cloned antiretroviral drugs to people with HIV/AIDS in Africa; that produces endless cars when the cities are already choked with vehicles; that prevents supermarkets from labelling foods in a way so people can see what they are eating.

Global share ownership

The transformation in the structure of ownership under globalisation expresses the process in a dynamic way. In 1981, investors from outside the UK owned just 3.1% of all the shares traded on the London stock exchange. By the end of 2006, this figure had shot up to 40% of traded shares, as the table below shows. UK individuals owned 13% of the shares in 2006 – compared with 28.2% in 1981 and a massive 54% in 1963. How the world has changed!

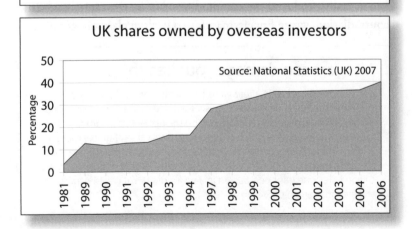

UK shares owned by overseas investors

Source: National Statistics (UK) 2007

Friedman received a Nobel Prize in 1976. His ideas gave expression to the current obsessions with unfettered operation of the competitive "free market", also known as neo-liberalism or the Washington Consensus. He was the spokesman for an agenda which has continued to inform the policies of governments and international agencies alike. But these guiding principles of capitalism were not introduced from outside. They aren't God-given. Friedman didn't invent them. They are built into the fabric of capitalist society, and are its very essence. Friedman just brought them out into the open, and restated them forcefully, at a time when capitalism was in trouble.

Karl Marx's work in analysing the nature of capitalism in the 19th century in *Das Kapital* revealed a system of production in which those who had accumulated wealth, largely through trade in slaves or by enclosing the land of family farmers, could use that capital to employ free workers and earn profits off the backs of their labour.[2]

The private ownership of the capital invested in infrastructure, machines, buildings and raw materials invariably comes into conflict with society's needs as well as the increasingly social nature of production itself based on high levels of co-operation by the workforce. Frederick Engels, Marx's great collaborator, explained this process well in *Anti-Dühring*, which was published in 1877. Engels explained how under capitalism "the owner of the instruments of labour always appropriated to himself the product, although it was no longer his product but exclusively the product of the labour of others. Thus, the products now produced socially were not appropriated by those who had actually set in motion the means of production and actually produced the commodities, but by the capitalists." This contradiction, wrote Engels, manifested itself in class antagonisms.

Mergers can damage your health

Between 1993 and 2004, there were 10,000 mergers and acquisitions in the American healthcare and drugs sector alone – a rate of almost 1,000 a year. US citizens are barred from buying their prescription drugs in Canada, where they are much cheaper. The total value of global merger and acquisition deals broke through the thousand billion dollar mark in the first three months of 2007. At $1,130bn, this is the first time that the $1 trillion milestone has been passed in a single quarter. It is a 14% jump on the first quarter of 2005.

Oligopoly Inc.

An oligopoly exists where a sector of the economy is in the hands of just a few corporations. The globalisation process has produced a consolidation of ownership that is staggering. According to the ETC Group, the world's 10 leading food processors and the top 10 food retailers now control a quarter of their multi-trillion dollar markets.

Between 2003 and 2005
- ▶ the world's top 10 seed companies increased their control from one-third to one half of the global seed trade
- ▶ the top 10 biotech enterprises raised their share from just over half to nearly three-quarters of world biotech sales
- ▶ the market share of the top 10 pesticide manufacturers rose modestly, from 80% to 84%; industry analysts predict that only three companies will survive the next decade
- ▶ the top 10 pharmaceutical companies accounted for 59% of total sales
- ▶ the top 100 food companies accounted for two-thirds of the global market share.

While workers co-operate across the globe in producing commodities and services, their products are placed on the market in a haphazard and chaotic way. This anarchic side of capitalism lies behind periodic disruptions to the international economy. As Engels said:

> No one knows how much of his particular article is coming on the market, nor how much of it will be wanted. No one knows whether his individual product will meet an actual demand, whether he will be able to make good his costs of production or even to sell his commodity at all.

These irreconcilable interests provide the inner dynamic of the development of society. They are the source of the recurrent and worsening crises experienced throughout the history of capitalist society, taking the violent forms of economic depression and slump and wars. These contradictions underlie the struggle between classes and social groups in society, leading to political challenge and change. They have driven fantastic technological advances but at a terrible price as we explain in Chapter 3.

In the search for profit, capitalist production tends to turn everything into a commodity for sale in the marketplace. Recent examples of new commodities include water supply, services like health and education, public transport and even governmental policy-making. These show how capitalist production emphasises the value that can be obtained from the sale of a commodity against its usefulness in satisfying needs.

As Marx revealed, a commodity has a use value because its physical characteristics can satisfy some human need or want. But it also has an exchange value, meaning that a commodity can be traded for other commodities, creating the conditions where profit can be made. Capitalism is basically concerned about exchange value above all other considerations.

Labour – the source of all value

Following many earlier economists, Marx showed that human labour is the source of all real value. However advanced technology is, no new value is added to a commodity without the labour of living human beings. But Marx went further, to show how capitalist society turned the ability to work itself into a commodity.

The owners of capital have a legally-binding contract with their employees. This contract requires the employee to sell their ability to work – their labour-power – to the employer for a specified period of time. Typically today, the employer is just as likely to be a Chinese or Indian sub-contractor of a transnational corporation as the TNC itself. In exchange, the employee gets paid wages or a salary, which is the price of the only commodity that an employee has for sale – his or her ability to work. The products that flow from the production process belong to the employer who sells them in the marketplace, at a profit. Bill Gates has become the richest man in the world by owning and selling the largely intellectual products of Microsoft's designers and programmers.

The heart of the whole process of making profit is the ability of workers – including managers – to add more value to inputs during the working day than the total cost of their employment. The hours of work specified in the employment contract between employer and employee ensure that the workers stay at work long enough to generate value above and beyond their own needs such as food, clothing and shelter paid out of their wage. This additional value is called surplus value. Like the rest of the value generated in the process, it is embedded in the products made. These, of course, belong to the employer.

A billion not enough

One billion dollars is no longer enough. The price of admission to the Forbes 400 of richest people, is now $1.3 billion, up $300 million from last year. The collective net worth of America's mightiest plutocrats rose $290 billion to $1.54 trillion. A total of 946 billionaires had an estimated combined wealth of $3.5 trillion.

For example, steel, glass, upholstery and other materials and components enter a car plant as a variety of inputs. Through the use of labour in the production process, they come out as higher value cars. The value added, which is the source of profit, comes from the hours of labour put in by the employees, managers, sub-contractors. They actively contribute to the production and distribution of the end-products which appear on the market. When the value of a commodity is realised by being exchanged for money in the market, it is distributed. The value of labour is paid to the workers. Part of surplus value is paid as rent to landowners. An increasingly significant part is paid as interest servicing debt, and a part is profit – which is the whole point of capitalist society – and is handed out to shareholders.

The falling rate of profit

The need to defend profits in an era of fierce competition pumps up the pressure to reduce the costs of production. These include machinery, commodities bought from suppliers, distribution including holding stock, and communications.

Obviously, reducing costs means paying less for inputs. This can be achieved in a number of ways, for example paying less for raw materials, or increasing the quantity of commodities produced by the same labour force. These productivity gains are made through capital investment, training to increase skills, and pushing employees into a longer working day or a faster/higher rate of working. Other ways to achieve the same result include cutting wages and benefits such as pensions and holiday pay, and by transfer of production to lower wage areas. Much of the drive to globalise production has come from these pressures.

Increasing productivity through capital investment drives down the rate of profit as fewer workers are available as the source of value, relative to the total amount invested. At the same time, increasing the volume of production reduces the cost and therefore the amount of value each commodity embodies. As price falls, many more units must be sold to maintain overall income. Growth therefore becomes absolutely essential in order to maintain let alone increase profits. This is the nub of the problem for capitalism. The corporations are constantly having to increase investment to run up the down escalator of reducing profits. This, as we show in Chapter 2, is why a credit orgy was released, only to turn into a credit crunch.

Intensifying productivity through new technology has paradoxical results. Jeremy Rifkin, author of 17 books on the impact of scientific and technological changes on society, and president of the Foundation on Economic Trends, has analysed how the globalised market economy tends to destroy jobs faster than they are created. According to Rifkin, in 1995, 800 million people were unemployed or underemployed. In 2004, more than a billion fell into one of these categories. In six years up to 2004, the US lost 12% of its factory jobs, while the UK shed 14% of its manufacturing jobs in the same period. Some 31 million manufacturing jobs were eliminated between 1995 and 2002 in the world's 20 largest economies. Manufacturing employment declined during a period when global industrial production rose by more than 30%. Rifkin said:

> If the current rate of decline continues – and it is more than likely to accelerate – manufacturing employment will dwindle from the current 164m jobs to just a few million by 2040, virtually ending the era of mass factory labour. Now the white-collar and services industries are experiencing similar job losses, as intelligent technologies replace more and more workers. Banking, insurance, and the wholesale and retail sectors are introducing smart technologies into every aspect of their business operations, fast eliminating support personnel in the process. The US internet banking company Netbank has $2.4bn in deposits. A typical bank that size employs 2,000 people. Netbank runs its entire operation with just 180 workers. (*Guardian*, 2 March 2004)

The old logic that technology gains and advances in productivity destroy old jobs but create as many new ones is no longer true, Rifkin argues. The US steel industry is typical of the transition taking place.

In the past 20 years, steel production rose from 75m tonnes to 102m tonnes. In the same period, from 1982 to 2002, the number of steelworkers in the US declined from 289,000 to 74,000. Rifkin adds:

> Herein lies the conundrum. If dramatic advances in productivity can replace more and more human labour, resulting in more workers being let go from the workforce, where will the consumer demand come from to buy all the potential new products and services? We are being forced to face up to an inherent contradiction at the heart of our market economy that has been present since the very beginning, but is only now becoming irreconcilable.

Overproduction

Production overcapacity is one of the hottest issues in the car industry today. Some industry observers claim that overcapacity is a myth, used by manufacturers as an excuse for closing plants in areas that are no longer important to them or that have become too expensive. But industry figures point to global overcapacity of about 20%. While overcapacity problems have been around for years, this has not stopped car makers from investing huge amounts of money in new plants around the world. Sales in the established markets of western Europe, the US and Japan have been slow for some time, and the emerging markets of Latin America, eastern Europe and Asia have been seen as offering the greatest potential for profitability and growth.

In South America, huge capacities were built in Brazil and Argentina in the 1990s. Much of this was left idle when the economies suffered at the end of the decade. Although sales are improving, they are well below the record levels of the 1990s and overcapacity remains an issue. China has been facing the same situation. Eager to position themselves for the widely anticipated growth of the Chinese market, all of the world's car makers invested massively in new plants. A new study by KPMG shows that while car sales in China remain strong, most industry commentators are concerned about overinvestment.

Andreas Dressles, *Foreign Direct Investment*

Overproduction

The corporations try whatever tactics they can think of to get us to buy more and more of their products. These may include cutting prices; making broadly equivalent products appear different and more attractive; bringing new products to the marketplace to satisfy unmet demands, and stimulating new demands; or undermining, weakening and then either buying up or finally destroying competitors.

The effect of the over-riding need to increase sales by selling ever greater volumes of ever cheaper products can be seen in the worldwide obesity pandemic, as well as in the surplus capacity in the car industry, and many others – particularly now in the East.

In May 2006, representatives of the US steel industry complained to the joint India/OECD/International Iron and Steel Institute meeting that Chinese and Indian government support was producing global overcapacity which "can lead to the well-known 'death spiral', in which producers race to cut prices while maintaining production". In a veiled threat they said:

> The construction of excess capacity in China and India will cost both countries billions of dollars in scarce capital. Overexpansion of the Chinese steel industry has already had negative effects on producers in the rest of the world; overexpansion of the Indian industry will only exacerbate the situation.

> Steel producers in both the developed and developing countries, including Brazil, have expressed concern over the building of excess capacity in these countries. Elimination of state support for the steel industry by China, India, and all other developing and developed countries is likely to limit excess capacity, and is more likely to result in a stable and healthy global steel industry.

Production inevitably reaches the limits of the market. People reach the limits of their disposable income. Savings are used up. Increased debt becomes unpayable as interest rates rise. Cars block the roads, ceasing to be useful means of transport. Monty Python's exploding Mr Creosote and his "wafer-thin mint" is a resonant symbol of over-production and its results.

Case study: India

Indian manufacturers are well known for their ability to be highly cost competitive - the cost of building a manufacturing plant in India is one-third of that in the US and Europe and the country also has a much lower cost of production and labour. Furthermore, by manufacturing in huge volumes, and thus creating an over capacity, Indian companies have managed to drive down prices. For example, the vaccines market has seen a phenomenal drop in prices in this way, according to Dr SV Kapre, executive director of the Serum Institute of India - the country's largest vaccines manufacturer. "In the US it typically costs $75 to make a vaccine dose, so that 10m doses costs $750m but in India it costs only $3 to make a 10 dose vial and so 10m doses costs only $3m," he said. As a result, the country currently dominates the world's active pharmaceutical ingredient (API) manufacturing arena - presently almost one in two APIs are now sourced in India and the market continues to grow.

Credit and consumption

As we explain in the next chapter, credit and debt extends the limits of consumption, enabling consumers to buy more. When these limits are reached, crisis, inflation, recession, slump, crash and the drive to war are set in motion.

The competition for raw materials and markets as capital expanded resulted in the 1914-18 world war between empires for control of territory. Post-war reconstruction encouraged increased industrialisation and new technologies, such as the radio, the car and air flight. The lure of profits from the boom – dividends from stock market investments – fed a euphoric rise on Wall Street and spawned a new industry of fraudulent companies, and inventive routes for speculation. The bubble burst with the 1929 crash and 90% of share values were destroyed by 1932. The whole world economy was affected. The Great Depression lasted until the build-up to the shattering destruction of the 1939-45 world war.

The post-1971 period of globalisation is the latest, most developed expression of capital's push for expansion. Under its influence the world economy is increasingly interconnected. The effects of each new crisis on the international markets are now transmitted instantly through the global networks.

Attempts to resolve the simultaneous stagnation and inflation of the 1970s through high interest rates produced a recession in the US in the early 1980s. Parallel deflationary policies imposed by the UK's Thatcher government from 1979 led quickly to a recession and a full-blown slump by 1985. Attempts to overcome this only led to a further recession in 1991-2. In October 1987, in the wake of a new slow-down in the US economy, several concurrent factors triggered a market crash. Accelerated and transmitted by the advent of computer-based trading over the internet, it marked the spread of the recession throughout most of the world. Its effects continued to be felt through to the middle of the 1990s.

Huge capital inflows into SE Asia in the 1980s and 1990s produced high growth rates which hit the buffers hard in 1997 as trade unions formed, strengthened and became increasingly militant. The financial crisis that reverberated around the world, with its epicentre in Thailand, erupted suddenly and viciously after declining growth revealed that many countries in the region had built unsustainably large piles of short-term external debt.

The effects of the financial crisis – seen in the 1998 collapse of hedge fund Long-Term Capital Management – interacted with the renewed, deepening global recession. Falling prices for raw materials undermined exporting countries including Russia. There was global disarray when the Russian government defaulted on its loans. The crisis continued to spread, to Latin America. The effects of "structural adjustment" and debt – market "solutions" imposed by the IMF and World Bank – provoked revolt and toppled governments, challenging the onward march of the corporations. From 1995 – just as in the early 1920s – the potential of new technologies, this time computing, telecommunications and telephony, seemed too good to ignore. Venture capitalists, flush with cash, ignited the speculative hysteria of the dot-com boom which crashed in March 2000.

Realisation that the wilder reaches of the boom had breached not only the limits of the market, but all boundaries of corporate governance came with the long-drawn out demise of Enron, Worldcom and a host of other huge corporations. A new period of growth began to emerge from the recession – which lasted until 2003 – after central banks' adopted low interest policies and governments reduced taxes to encourage business. The factors that created the 1997 Asian crisis reappeared there in earnest in 2006, as GDP continued its 2005 decline[3]. Signs of recession also began to appear in the US, the biggest consumer in the world. The impact of the crisis on the advanced, but declining over-developed economies of the West, so long delayed, began to emerge.

Today, the unfolding crisis goes much deeper. Global production capacity by far exceeds available markets. Propelled by a reckless, uncontrolled credit explosion, the global economy is heading for the buffers.

References

1. United Nations Conference on Trade and Development (UNCTAD), World Investment Report 2007

2. Marx, Karl. *Das Kapital*
http://www.marxists.org/archive/marx/works/1867-c1/index.htm

3. Economic crisis closing in on South Korea, *Asia Times* online, 22 February 2007
http://www.atimes.com/atimes/Korea/IB22Dg01.html

2

The spectre haunting capitalism

In the summer of 2007, the institutions operating in the world's financial system suffered what the *Financial Times* described as a heart attack. A "credit crunch" ended a long and immensely profitable period in which financial traders in shiny glass and steel towers amassed huge personal wealth by playing global markets.

The endless supply of new and exciting financial "products" delivering high returns using other peoples' money, was exposed as a massive illusion. Commentators began using the dreaded "C" words – capitalism and crash – which governments like New Labour had derided as "so last century".

It took almost a decade from the series of financial shocks in Asia and Russia for the debt crisis to make its sudden appearance in the United States, the world's largest economy. Thereafter, the crisis has assumed a global character and an unpredictable course and the new financial instruments have played a key role in its unfolding.

The expansion and transformation of the corporation has defined the period of capitalist globalisation. It fed off and accelerated the technological revolution in communications. But unprecedented financial investment was needed to develop and promote this transformation. The deluge of money and credit helped to create the myth that the world of finance functioned independently from the production of goods and services.

Earlier occurrences of this phenomenon were observed by Karl Marx in the 19th century. His analysis of the role of credit under capitalism shows how the buying and selling of the rights to own debt, and more importantly the interest payments due on it – a process he called "the formation of a fictitious capital" – leads to a peculiar situation. Under these conditions, "all connection with the actual expansion process of capital is thus completely lost, and the conception of capital as something with automatic self-expansion properties is thereby strengthened".

In *Das Kapital*, Marx remarks:

> With the development of interest-bearing capital and the credit system, all capital seems to double itself, and sometimes treble itself, by the various modes in which the same capital, or perhaps even the same claim on a debt, appears in different forms in different hands. The greater portion of this 'money-capital' is purely fictitious.

As in the past, the expansion of credit was founded on the belief and expectation that the real economy – and therefore profits from it – would continue to grow, enabling future earnings to service interest on the mounting debts. When that ended, so did the game of financial musical chairs. Now the spectre haunting global capitalism is the unravelling of the mountains of debt that were piled up during this process.

Speculators have created pyramids of debt out of exotic, derivative financial products. The longer that real growth continued, the greater their confidence soared. Fatally, increased confidence bred a growing appetite for risk and ever wilder fantasies. Their fervent belief in their own fantastic creations was reinforced by success. For a while the speculators blinded the rest of the world as well. They spent some of their money on property, driving prices up around the world. They sold people mortgages which are dependent on property prices continuing to rise and rise and rise. By repackaging and recycling debt, they created the myth that their fragile creations reduced risk by spreading it throughout the economy.

As Anthony Hilton, business editor of the London *Evening Standard* observed:

> Under the influence of globalisation, the nature of financial markets has changed. They came into existence originally to facilitate trade, spread risk, create markets and provide skills to aid the efficient functioning of what we used quaintly to call the real economy. Now finance is an end in itself it no longer needs a real economy to function, because it has gone off into hyperspace, operating in a virtual world, using the derivative markets to create its own virtual money and only occasionally touching down in the world the rest of us inhabit not unlike Viking raiders coming ashore for a quick bit of rape and pillage before making off again. (7 August 2007)

Fittingly, the financial system began to unravel in the land of dreams itself – the United States of America. In the wake of 17 consecutive interest rate rises imposed by the Federal Reserve – America's central bank – in an attempt to reduce inflation, a rash of mortgage defaults by low-income borrowers began to accumulate, eventually driving the largest of the home loan companies into bankruptcy. By the end of 2005, the housing market in some US states came to a standstill. The "sub-prime" crisis was born, eventually leading to a global "credit crunch". Historically unprecedented loose conditions for credit dried up. The crisis spread rapidly as the reciprocal effect of the global financial markets started to wreak havoc throughout the global economy.

The US housing crisis is, however, an indication of something much more profound. The essential growth in US consumption, upon which much of the rest of the world's production depended, had already passed its peak and was declining, slowing down from a 4% average until the first quarter of 2007 to a weak 1.3% in the second quarter.

In the UK, mortgage lender Northern Rock, heavily dependent on the seized-up financial market for credit to finance its own lending business, plunged into deep crisis as its liquidity dried up. Savers, sensing the impending loss of their deposits queued to withdraw their money in the first run on a British high street bank for 150 years. Ten years earlier Northern Rock, like many other building societies, had given up its mutual status, falling for the lure of bigger profits. The queues that gathered in September 2007 were the first signs of the long financial winter to come.

The origins of credit

Money evolved historically because of the need for a special commodity which could act as the measure of value needed to facilitate the exchange in the marketplace.[1] It removed the constraint that barter imposed on direct exchange of commodities. People could now sell what they had, obtaining its value in the form of money, without immediately having to buy something else. In this early form, commodities used as money themselves had value, because they too were the products of labour. Examples included cows, and pigs. [The English words *"capital"*, *"chattels"* and *"cattle"* have a common root. Similarly *"pecuniary"* comes from the Latin word for cattle *"pecus"*.]

To allow the development of international trade on a large scale, money commodities needed to be small enough to be portable, infinitely divisible and of little use for other purposes. Most importantly they should be the product of measurable quantities of labour. Of all the metals used for this purpose, silver and finally gold were adopted as the universal standard which lasted, with interruptions, until 1971.

As manufacture grew, it began to make accelerating demands on raw materials located in distant countries. The periods of time involved in sending out a request, the despatch of the raw materials and their arrival and use in production introduced new delays compared with the original face-to-face marketplace exchanges.

Credit, which is the separation between purchase of a commodity and payment for it, developed as the means of managing these distant social relationships. Instead of carrying gold or silver coins to pay for goods before they were received, the traders carried promises to pay written on paper – bills of exchange – adopting and developing credit transfer practices developed by the Greeks in the second and third centuries BC. The supplier of the raw materials had to take the promise to pay on trust. He had to have confidence in the developing credit system.

In the 21st century, bills of exchange have been replaced by complex financial derivatives that have only an electronic existence in global virtual networks. Today, the expansion of credit and debt issued by unregulated finance houses is calculated using mathematical models manipulated by computers. Here money appears to be made from money, from interest, the charge made for its use until the promise to pay bears fruit. Torrents of credit and debt flow around the international networks between banks, through share markets and investment banks, providing the funds for worldwide investments by corporations, commodity trades, mergers, takeovers, acquisitions and private equity deals. These financial instruments recycle shareholdings, savings, and pension funds. The whole system is fed by currencies issued by government-controlled national central banks, and supplied through wholesale markets operated by and between commercial banks.

Global financial operators including credit card companies like Visa and Mastercard, hedge fund managers and mortgage lenders supply yet more credit. Speculators engage in ever-riskier financial deals with the hope of making a profit. Their activities depend – and feed on – a much faster expansion of credit than even the wildest hopes of growth in the real economy producing goods and services.

This world of fantasy finance gives the impression that the whole system of credit has floated free of reality. But the truth is that all this credit surging through the system depends in the end on the promise of profits from continuous growth – and consumption – in the real economy. When growth falters, the "promise to pay" can no longer stand up, and confidence is undermined. Lenders increase interest rates to reflect risk, or reduce or stop lending altogether, preferring to hoard what they know they have. Credit flow becomes credit crunch. When this happens, as it did in the summer of 2007, when commercial banks stopped transacting business on the wholesale markets, economic activity starts to grind to a halt.

The Big Bang

The expansion of credit remains healthy – so long as it remains in line with the growth of the real economy measured by Gross Domestic Product (GDP). Conversely, the more credit is issued, whether paper or electronic, the less it is worth if GDP fails to grow at the same pace. This is the source of price inflation. As the quantity of paper money and other forms of credit grows in relation to the value of things it can buy, its value declines. Each pound or dollar or yen can buy less than before.

And what this means today is that the amount of new value produced in relation to the volumes of credit issued in the recent period is extremely small.

In 1980, the world's financial assets were valued at 108% of the value of annual production, more or less in line with each other. But just 25 years later, the ratio had widened dramatically. The IMF estimates that in 2005 the total value of global financial assets, comprising banking assets, stock market capitalisation and bond market value, amounted to US$165 trillion – nearly **four times** the size of global GDP of US$45 trillion. This vastly increased quantity of finance was never destined to sit quietly in deposit accounts. In 1980, bank deposits made up 42% of all financial securities. By 2005, this had fallen to 27%. The other 73% of deposits were set in motion, swirling through the new global computer networks of the capital markets and investment banks to fuel corporate development.

Investors looking for more profitable places for their capital looked abroad. They opened channels into new countries, enabling corporations to leap across continents, mutating to multinational and then transnational status. None of this was possible whilst capital controls and regulations on the financial sector in and between countries remained in place. So tight national controls on banks, investment and insurance companies, and on the operation of international markets in currencies and capital, were swept away.

Deregulation began in Britain as soon as the Tories came to power in 1979. One of Margaret Thatcher's first acts as prime minister was to abolish currency exchange controls, paving the way for foreign banks to compete with their British rivals and with the stock market as it enabled money to move freely in and out of Britain. In 1983, the government and the stock exchange drew up a new framework which brought electronic trading to the City and instantly did away with face-to-face share deals and restrictions on equity dealing.

A financial 'monster'

The result is that the notional value of these financial products in, for example, the complex world of credit derivatives is many times greater than the value of the entire world gross national product. And because these products are virtual, created by human ingenuity there is no limit on how much they can grow or how big the business can become…

The only constraint is complexity, and the only limit on that is available computing power and the human imagination both of which have a very long way to go. The huge danger, however, is that like Frankenstein, our ability to create financial monsters is highly likely to outstrip our ability to control them.

Anthony Hilton, business editor *Evening Standard*, 7 August 2007

The new regime came into force on 27 October 1986 and transformed the City: the value of traded shares increased by **1,500%**, from £161bn in 1986 to £2,496bn in 2006, while banking sector assets increased by a factor of seven to £5,500bn. The change-over was known as the Big Bang. It certainly was for the traditional merchant banks and City brokers – they have long disappeared, replaced by global investment banks and brokerages like Goldman Sachs and Credit Suisse.

Cross-border controls on capital movements gave way to foreign direct investment as the motor of growth, feeding first the South East Asian economies, then the phenomenal expansion of production in China, India and Mexico. On the way, currency speculators played a big role in driving many developing countries into economic crisis. The International Monetary Fund and World Bank stepped in, offering loans on the condition that these countries open their markets to foreign investment. Repayments on the loans became an increasing burden on the already impoverished populations, soaking up more and more of GDP, and creating a new form of colonialism – debt colonialism.

Wage-earners pay more tax

In Britain, New Labour under Gordon Brown has cut corporation tax so that at 28% the rate will be the lowest of the major economies; it was 52% in 1982. Corporate profits as a share of GDP have increased on average from 21.5% to 22.5% since 1999, the proportion paid in corporation tax has fallen from 15% to 14.1%, according to the Tax Justice Network (TJN). At the same time, the majority of UK ordinary earners have seen the share of their income taken by tax and national insurance rise to around 30%.

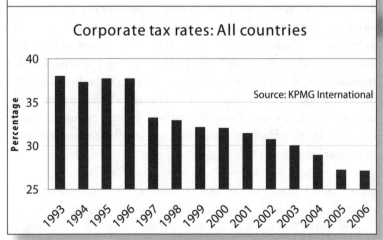

Corporate tax rates: All countries

Source: KPMG International

Deriving a profit

The swelling volume of finance needed to fuel the growth of commodity production could not be contained within the traditional forms of government bonds, equities, commodities and foreign exchange. Greedy and reckless speculators could not resist the prospects of unregulated profits on offer. Investment banks recruited skilled mathematicians to invent an array of new, highly complex products which further expanded the seemingly limitless inflation of finance capital.

Among the best-known of these "derivatives" – so called because they were built on the back of the old forms – are options, futures and swaps. By the end of 2006 the outstanding value of interest rate swaps, currency swaps and interest rate options had reached $286,000bn – about six times global gross product.

The structure of the markets and the vast sums on the move expose all participants to risk of almost unimaginable proportions. The interconnectedness of the global markets greatly intensifies the potential effects of contagion.

On the back of the derivatives markets came yet another layer of actors: the hedgers and speculators. Operating in a new, therefore unregulated marketplace, they gambled on the volatility that accompanied the newly-minted capital.

The largest market of all is in foreign currency speculation. This erupted into life to support the operations of multinational corporations. Its traders derive their fortunes from fluctuating exchange rates. Speculators bet on the smallest movements – up or down – in currencies. They buy and sell electronically, their trading screens operating around the clock. Trading houses never sleep – as the Tokyo market closes, London's opens. In the year to April 2006, overall turnover on the foreign exchange markets averaged around **US$2.9 trillion** a day. That's around 60 times the value of the world's GDP for the **whole year**, and more than ten times the size of the combined daily turnover on all the world's equity markets. Foreign exchange trading increased by 38% between April 2005 and April 2006 and has more than doubled since 2001.[2]

Case study: Sallie Mae

The credit crunch has begun to take its toll on private equity ventures. Sallie Mae was established in 1972 as a US government-sponsored corporation to finance student loans, and was privatised in 2004. It made $23.4bn in new loans in 2006. In April 2007, JC Flowers & Co, a private equity firm launched a bid to buy the corporation and acquire debt of around $153bn owed by 10 million students. In October 2007, in the wake of the global credit crisis, it reduced its $25bn offer to $21bn, an estimated 16% downgrade in the value of debt.

Private equity

Private equity companies have come to prominence as the modern version of asset-strippers. Companies like Blackstone, Apax Partners and Permira, which are not listed on stock exchanges, deploy huge funds borrowed from financial markets. In a relentless search for new sources of value, these unregulated private equity firms turn companies into commodities.

They buy out publicly-quoted companies, converting them into private enterprises. Once in the shadows, away from the glare of stock market accountability, their purchases are stripped of valuable, but inessential assets, while large numbers of jobs are eliminated.

With the promise of large and continuing returns on the capital invested, the private equity funds attract subscribers lured by the promise of big returns. In the process, well-known companies like Debenhams, the AA, Chrysler, Sainsbury's, and Boots were targeted.

Having finished their task, the equity fund managers sell the company on, taking huge management fees and profits from the sale. From then on, the first call on any surplus made by the revitalised company is used to service the debt, paying the interest on the loans that were used to buy the company in the first place! This trick neatly turns taxable profit into a tax-deductible cost.

For example, the AA – the roadside recovery chain – paid almost no corporation tax in 2005 and 2006. Loaded down with debt under private equity ownership, its operating profits were almost entirely consumed by interest payments. CVC and Permira have also slashed the workforce. The GMB union said that £70m of the AA's £200m profits in 2006 were attributable to the 3,400 cuts in its workforce of 10,000 when it came under private equity control. The managing partner of Permira is Damon Buffini. He is now an official advisor to the New Labour government.

Government-run investment pools in the Middle East and Asia known as sovereign wealth funds have also grown rapidly and given rise to a new twist of global finance, and new threads of interconnection. The growth of exports from China and other emerging economies – particularly those that export commodities including oil and essential mined minerals – has caused these funds to soar. These countries have accumulated a vast and growing pool of foreign exchange, much larger than the sums controlled by hedge funds and private equity groups.

Newly rich countries including China, Russia, Dubai and even Norway began to recycle this accumulating wealth through sovereign wealth funds. These were used to acquire foreign firms, invest in property, or on stock markets, or higher-yielding corporate bonds.[3] They also bought into US national debt to the point where an estimated 44% is under foreign control, with a large proportion in the hands of the Chinese government.

Personal and household credit and debt

Whilst the liberalised, turbo-charged, globally-networked financial markets enabled new, more efficient and productive corporate forms to break free of national constraints, they began to encounter new limits. With substantial capital investment in hugely profitable businesses with cheap labour in Asia and Latin America, the mass production of ever-cheaper commodities skyrocketed.

Credit cards

More than 1 million people use high-interest credit cards to cover their mortgage or rent payments, debt experts say. Six per cent of householders have turned to plastic to pay for the roof over their heads during the past year, according to housing charity Shelter. Young people struggling to stay on the property ladder are most likely to use the 'rob Peter to pay Paul tactics', despite risking long-term ruin. Many credit card companies charge interest between 15 and 18 per cent – up to three times higher than typical mortgage rates.

Metro, 16 October 2007

But the globalising corporations' use of exported capital to exploit cheap labour helped to reduce the real value of wages worldwide and hence the purchasing power of people in the developed economies. A decline in the developed countries' ability to absorb the increasing mass of commodities became apparent. Conditions had to be provided for the personal credit and debt industry to develop as the means to start and keep the spending binge rolling.

Central banks kept interest rates low to encourage borrowing. Mortgages were made available cheaply so property prices ballooned. House-builders in the US, in Spain and in other parts of the world responded to the increased demand that arose from easily available credit. Lenders invented new, unregulated channels to supply credit, notably to the sub-prime market, comprising people with little or no security or documented proof of income.

Throughout the world, personal credit limits were raised and debt grew exponentially. The wide-eyed expectation of ever-increasing property prices encouraged lenders to offer mortgages larger even than 100% of the price of the property, so that borrowers could furnish their new homes with brand new imports from the Chinese white goods production lines. And the mortgage-to-income ratio was allowed to widen to as much as five, six or even 10 times. Individuals and households spent their savings as consumption remained high despite relative earnings falling throughout the richer countries of the OECD.

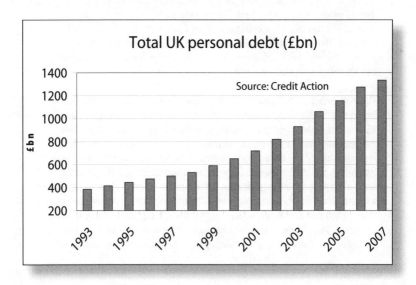

Total UK personal debt (£bn)

Source: Credit Action

Debt in the UK

In the UK, personal debt as a proportion of annual national income rose from 105% in 1997 to 164% in 2006 – this was the highest yet recorded and the biggest in the developed world. Having soared from £400 million in 1993, by the end of June 2007 the total amount of outstanding UK consumer debt, amassed through mortgages, loans and credit card balances reached £1,345 billion. This exceeded the amount generated by the UK economy, estimated at around £1,330 billion. This was the first time that the country's 60 million people owed more to the banks than the value of everything made by every office and factory in the country in a year.

Total secured lending on homes at the end of July 2007 stood at £1,140bn, an increase of 11% in just 12 months. The average amount outstanding for the 11.8m households with mortgages reached £96,560. The number of mortgages in arrears of three months or more at the end of June 2007 rose to an estimated 125,100, up 4% compared with the end of December 2006.

Some 14,000 properties (77 a day) were repossessed in the first six

Prime suspect

According to a BBC Panorama investigation in October 2007, sub-prime mortgage lenders who give loans to people with bad credit records account for more than 70% of all repossessions, even higher than in the US where the figure is 55%. The market for high interest sub-prime mortgages has been booming and it now accounts for about 8% of the total UK mortgage market. The investigation found cases of council tenants on benefits encouraged to exaggerate their incomes to be able to buy their houses under the right-to-buy.

The BBC explored the case of David and Maureen Bradbury, who despite being in their late 50s, on benefits and in poor health, were given a 25-year mortgage worth £55,000 by London Scottish Bank. With their interest rate over 11%, they are struggling to make repayments and face repossession. Many banks and building societies involved in sub-prime lending in the UK bundle up hundreds of mortgages like the Bradbury's and sell them to investors for cash up front. This trade in debt has become a multi-billion pound industry in the City of London and many investors – including pension funds – have eagerly bought a piece of this market. Whoever is left holding the debt may be playing a game of pass-the-parcel where the parcel is worthless when the final wrapper comes off.

months of 2007, up 18% on the previous half-year and 30% higher than the first half of 2006. There has been a sharp slowdown in mortgage lending in the UK says the Council of Mortgage Lenders (CML). Gross lending dipped by 12% from August to September 2007, to £30bn. Although still higher than in September last year, the drop from month to month was larger than is usually seen at this time of year. The CML said it was another sign that the housing market was responding to the five increases in interest rates since the summer of 2006, exactly mirroring what happened last year in the United States.

According to research by the Conservative Social Justice Policy Group between seven and nine million people in Britain have had a serious debt problem and they estimate that British consumers are on average twice as indebted as those in Continental Europe.[4]

The great unravelling

Some claim that credit and debt can be permanently separated from the "real economy", and have an independent existence. This is wishful thinking. All the evidence reveals quite the opposite – a relationship of mutual dependency between productive capital and fictitious capital. The consequences of the "credit crunch" and crisis in global financial markets are now being felt throughout the productive economy in terms of jobs, pensions and repossessions.

Each year since 1978, the Federal Reserve Bank of Kansas City has sponsored a symposium at Jackson Hole in Wyoming on an important economic issue facing the US and world economies. Symposium participants include prominent central bankers, finance ministers, academics, and financial market players from around the world. This year the subject, fittingly, was housing, housing finance and monetary policy.

The summing up on 1 September by Martin Feldstein, president and chief executive officer, National Bureau of Economic Research, made gloomy reading. As far as the US economy was concerned, Feldstein pointed to:

▶ a 3.4% decline in housing prices over the past 12 months and an estimated 9% annual rate of decline in the most recent month for which data were available

▶ a collapse in home building, down 20% from a year ago, to the lowest level in a decade; such declines in housing construction were a precursor to eight of the past 10 recessions

▶ a warning that a 20% decline in house prices would cut wealth by some $4 trillion and might cut consumer spending by $200 billion or about 1.5% of GDP.

Financial Times columnist Martin Wolf's assessment of the UK housing sector makes equally chilling reading. Wolf, who is an expert on globalisation, wrote on 4 October 2007:

> Why might the UK go the way of the US? The answer is that it has very similar vulnerabilities: house prices are high by any standards; in the second quarter of 2007, household saving was only 3.1% of disposable income; as house prices have soared, so has residential investment, which has reached 10% of disposable income, up from just 5.5% six years ago; and the overall household financial deficit is, in consequence, at the record level of 7% of disposable income.

> If US households are sinking in debt, UK households seem to be drowning in it. All this strongly suggests the possibility of house price weakness and a sharp reduction in the household financial deficit. While corporate balance sheets are strong, business investment would surely weaken if household consumption did. This would seem a recipe for a slowdown, possibly even a recession.

In the light of these two assessments the economic fundamentals, as capitalist agencies like the IMF like to call them, look far from sound. In fact, the IMF in October warned that house prices in the UK could also collapse, a view echoed by Alan Greenspan, former head of the Federal Reserve in Washington.

The not-so-almighty dollar

In mid-September of 2007 a US congressional panel heard that "the collapse of home prices might turn out to be the most severe since the Great Depression". Within hours of the hearings, the Federal Reserve took panic action and slashed interest rates by 0.5% in an attempt to

Terrifying speed

The first crisis to test the new world of finance showed that the markets are so inter-connected and so global that that the poison can spread across markets and continents with terrifying speed.
The Economist 20 October 2007

Contagion will spread

Finally, is this the end of the story of crisis and contagion? "Far from it" is my guess. If we can have such trouble with the financial system when the real economy is healthy, I tremble at what may happen when conditions start to become worse. The financial system looks more insecure than I feared. The unwinding of past excesses may well bring more unpleasant surprises. But it is necessary, and healthy, all the same.
Martin Wolf, *Financial Times* 18 September 2007

Spooked

Depositors were naturally spooked themselves when the same government that had promised them victory in Iraq said their money was safe. The rush to withdraw savings was exacerbated by the formation of queues, as Pavlovian a lure to Britons as an "eat all you can for a fiver" sign outside a burger bar.
Jonathan Guthrie, *Financial Times* 20 September 2007

Dollar crisis

If Ben Bernanke [head of the US Federal Reserve] starts running those printing presses even faster than he's already doing, we are going to have a serious recession. The dollar's going to collapse, the bond market's going to collapse. There's going to be a lot of problems.
Commodity trader Jim Rogers, *Daily Telegraph* 20 September 2007

Next in line

The next big question is who will follow Northern Rock into the casualty ward. An awful lot of people on the inside expect another bailout. While the laws of libel stop me naming the suspects, it is not difficult to do a trawl of banks whose loan books seem to have expanded much faster than their deposit base in recent years. They may get through by massive belt-tightening and regular Hail Mary's but I would not count on it.
Anthony Hilton, *Evening Standard* 27 September 2007

resuscitate the American economy to stave off recession.

For the money markets, as well as those countries like Saudi Arabia loaded down with dollar bills, the rate cut was a signal that perhaps this was the right time to cut and run – and the dollar's value plummeted. Most of world trade is conducted in dollars so a collapse in its value, combined with a credit crunch, will intensify the crisis.

Historically, the Saudis have linked their currency to the dollar and have always matched US interest rate movements. Not this time, however. The Saudis' refusal to cut their own rates was taken as a signal that the oil-rich feudal kingdom is preparing to break with the dollar in favour of the euro. "This is a very dangerous situation for the dollar," said Hans Redeker, currency chief at investment bank BNP Paribas. "Saudi Arabia has $800 billion in their future generation fund, and the entire region has $3,500 billion under management. They face an inflationary threat and do not want to import an interest rate policy set for the recessionary conditions in the United States," he said.

As if that was not enough, in August the Chinese government started a concerted campaign of economic threats against the United States, hinting that it may liquidate its vast holding of US treasury bonds if Washington imposes trade sanctions to force a revaluation of the yuan.

There is also evidence that global investors, with no national allegiances, are shunning the US bond markets. By gradually pulling out of the long-term market in US debt they are leaving the dollar dependent on short-term funding. "This is nothing like the situation in 1998 when the crisis was in Asia, but the US was booming. This time the US itself is the problem," Redeker said.

In 1929 the stock market frenzy ended in the Wall Street Crash, ushering in the slump and depression of the 1930s. Capitalism could only restart its growth path after destroying surplus capacity on a scale previously unimaginable. That was achieved by the bombing raids and blitzkriegs of the Second World War. Today, the magnitude of debt swirling around the global economy means that the crisis is far deeper than 1929. Decades of intense globalisation have drawn every part of the world into a single interconnected whole. The multiple causes and consequences of the credit crunch do not just occur in one country and are transmitted around the world. They occur simultaneously in every continent.

References

1. Marx, Karl. *Capital* Volume 1, Chapter 3: Money, or the circulation of commodities, http://www.marxists.org/archive/marx/works/1867-c1/ch03.htm

2. What keeps bankers awake at night? *The Economist*. 1 February 2007 http://economist.com/finance/displaystory.cfm?story_id=8633485

3. Nouriel Roubini, *Bogeymen of Financial Capitalism*, http://www.koreatimes.co.kr/www/news/opinon/2007/09/137_9462.html

4. For the first time, Britons' personal debt exceeds Britain's GDP, *Independent*, 24 August 2007, http://money.independent.co.uk/personal_finance/loans_credit/article2891207.ece

5. Credit Action, http://www.creditaction.org.uk/debtstats.htm

6. Ibid

3

Paying the price

In four decades of unplanned, unregulated, profit-driven growth, corporate-driven globalisation has:

▶ initiated and intensified a period of rapid climate change that is undermining the conditions for life on the planet
▶ dramatically widened the gulf between the vastly wealthy few and the billions condemned to struggle for survival
▶ induced a culture of extreme consumerism directly responsible for the global obesity pandemic
▶ trapped individuals, companies and countries with unrepayable debt
▶ launched illegal wars for resources and markets, obliterating infrastructure, sparking genocide and mass migration
▶ replaced parliamentary democracy with authoritarian rule.

Climate Change

The International Panel on Climate Change (IPCC), representing the consensus views of the world's scientific community, published three reports early in 2007.[1] In the words of the IPCC:

> Global atmospheric concentrations of carbon dioxide, methane and
> nitrous oxide have increased markedly as a result of human activities
> since 1750 and now far exceed pre-industrial values determined from
> ice cores spanning many thousands of years. The global increases in
> carbon dioxide concentration are due primarily to fossil fuel use
> and land-use change, while those of methane and nitrous oxide are
> primarily due to agriculture.[2]

Through intense lobbying on behalf of the most powerful corporations, political influence brought to bear on the scientists who comprise the IPCC obliged them to use the vague, neutral term "human activities". The 250 years of "activities" referred to by the IPCC begins with the introduction of factory production, the new economy of industrial capitalism.

Carbon dioxide is the most important greenhouse gas. The global atmospheric concentration of carbon dioxide has increased from a pre-industrial value of about 280 parts per million (ppm) to 379ppm in 2005. The atmospheric concentration of carbon dioxide in 2005 exceeds by far the natural range over the last 650,000 years (180 to 300ppm) as determined from ice cores. But what is most significant is that according to the IPCC, the annual CO_2 growth rate was larger during the last 10 years (1995 – 2005 average: 1.9ppm per year), than it has been since the beginning of continuous direct atmospheric measurements (1960 – 2005 average: 1.4ppm per year).

In other words, the recent increase in the rate of concentration of CO_2 exactly parallels the acceleration in globalisation which occurred in the 1990s. Despite global awareness of their impact on the climate, emissions of CO_2 and many other pollutants from corporate, profit-led growth continue to intensify and accelerate climate change. At the end of August 2005, Hurricane Katrina delivered a devastating shock to the city and people of New Orleans. In November 2007, the entire Mexican state of Tabasco – the size of Belgium – was overwhelmed by flood waters. These are early warnings of the scale and impact of climate change.

Leading scientific institutions see the 21st century as the biggest period of mass extinction in the history of life on the planet. Unchecked, the explosive, poisonous growth of commodity production and consumption is destroying animal and plant species. As a 2006 report

Case study: Australia

Sheep and cattle farmer Ian Shippen stands in a dying ankle-high oat crop under a mobile irrigation boom stretching nearly half-a-kilometre, but now useless without water. "I honestly think we're stuffed," he says grimly.

"It's on a knife edge and if it doesn't rain in the next couple of weeks it's going to be very ugly. People will be walking off the land, going broke." Shippen's property "Chah Singh" sits in the heart of Australia's Murray-Darling river basin, a vast plain bigger than France and Germany, home to 2 million people and in good times the source of almost half the nation's fruit and cereal crop.

But years of drought, which some blame on global warming, have savagely depleted the huge dams built 60 years ago to hold the snow melt from the Australian alps and push it hundreds of kilometres inland to the parched west for farm irrigation.

The Murray-Darling normally provides 90% of Australia's irrigated crops and A\$22 billion (\$18.1 billion) worth of agricultural exports to Asia and the Middle East. But with some crops now just 10 days from failure, farmers are to receive no water at all for irrigation through the summer, while others will get a fraction of their regular entitlement to keep alive vital plantings like citrus trees and grapevines.

The massive Hume Weir, which can hold enough water to fill seven Sydney Harbours, is so dry that a lakeside holiday village is now half-a-kilometre from the depleted shore and rods to measure water depth stand on bare rock far from the waters' edge. "It's grim. The water is not there," says Wendy Craik, the head of the Murray-Darling Basin Commission which oversees storage in the country's longest river and dam system.'[4]
Reuters, 29 August 2007

in *Nature* magazine put it: "Virtually all aspects of biodiversity are in steep decline and a large number of populations and species are likely to become extinct this century."

In the same year, the UK government's Stern Report into the economic impact of global warming, and to find ways of enabling growth to continue, revealed that climate change will reduce welfare by an amount equivalent to a reduction in consumption of as much as 20%.[3]

Stern described climate change as "the greatest and widest-ranging market failure ever seen". In other words, the global system of capitalist production and distribution is responsible for wrecking the planet's ecosystems. It is responsible for global warming and climate change which is already having a reciprocal, devastating impact on the economy.

The scientific observations used in the IPCC's painstaking analytical work were, inevitably, two years behind the accelerating crisis. Later reports showed that polar ice was melting much faster than the models used by the IPCC predicted.

Wild weather events multiplied. Monsoon rains were the worst ever, displacing tens of millions of people in China and India. Unprecedented floods in Northern Europe put towns and cities underwater, and damaged crops. Southern Europe sweltered. Fires swept Greece and North America; East Africa was hit by floods.

Despite irrefutable evidence and a global scientific consensus about the source of global warming, its impact on climate change and the consequences for the economy, burning of fossil fuels looks set to spiral upwards. China's voracious demand for energy to feed its booming economy has led it to seek oil supplies from African countries including Sudan, Chad, Nigeria, Angola, Algeria, Gabon, Equatorial Guinea, and the Republic of Congo. China opens a new coal-fired power station every **week**.

The increase in global-warming gases from China's coal use will probably exceed that for all industrialised countries combined over the next 25 years, surpassing by five times the reduction in such emissions that the Kyoto Protocol seeks.[5]

The sulphur dioxide produced by coal combustion poses an immediate threat to the health of China's citizens, contributing to about 400,000 premature deaths a year. It also causes acid rain that poisons lakes, rivers, forests and crops.

Meanwhile, an international agreement to cut greenhouse gas emissions is beyond reach because the global corporations and compliant governments cannot get off the growth treadmill. There are no market-led solutions to climate chaos. The global rush to biofuels will actually increase emissions of greenhouse gases and is leading to higher food prices. The growing market in carbon itself has created a deadly opportunity to create more profits without reducing emissions at all.

Inequality at home and abroad

Inequality has widened at the fastest rate ever in this rapid, intense period of corporate-driven globalisation. According to the most comprehensive study of personal wealth ever undertaken,[6] in 2000 the richest 2% of adults in the world owned more than half of global household wealth, the richest 1% of adults alone owned 40% of global assets, and the richest 10% of adults accounted for 85% of the world total. In contrast, the bottom half of the world adult population owned barely 1% of global wealth.

Reports published in 2007 by the Joseph Rowntree Foundation (JRF) reveal inequality in Britain is at a 40-year high. The JRF findings do not delve into socio-economic causes. But their conclusions speak for themselves because the period studied – 1968 to 2005 – coincides with the contemporary globalisation period.

Researchers discovered that households in already-wealthy areas have tended to become disproportionately wealthier and that many rich people live in areas segregated from the rest of society. At the same time, more households have become poor over the last 15 years. The widening gap between rich and poor has meant that "average" households (neither poor nor wealthy) have been decreasing in number. A second report studied people's attitudes to inequality. It found that over the last 20 years, a large and enduring majority of people have considered the gap between high and low incomes too large.

According to government statistics, in 2004, over 20% of the UK population were officially income poor compared with 13% when New Labour came to office. These figures include 3.5 million children and 3 million pensioners. Twice as many people are homeless compared to 1997. In 1986 in the UK, the richest 1% held 25% of marketable wealth; by 2006 National Statistics estimated this had risen to 34%.

Meanwhile, the poorest 50% went from holding 11% of the nation's wealth in 1986 to just 1% today. In 1996 the wealthiest 5% of the population owned 49% of wealth; by 2003 this had risen to 58%. Executive pay has risen by 288% in the decade since 1993, and in 2006 alone rose by 28% – seven times the increase in average pay. As inequality has risen in the UK so the odds have lengthened of overcoming socio-economic background. Research by the LSE shows that social mobility has declined over the last 30 years.

The era of globalisation has also intensified inequalities between rich and poor, both globally and within nations. Half of the world's population lives on less than $2 per day. The combined income of the world's 48 poorest nations is less than the wealth of the world's three richest people. The 20% of us living in the richest countries consume nearly 90% of global resources. Poverty kills 30,000 children every day, a death rate far exceeding the worst genocides or wars.

How has this disparity in wealth and mobility come about? In December 2006, after 30 years of globalisation, Stephen S. Roach, managing director and chief economist of Morgan Stanley, a leading global financial services firm, gave his assessment:

> At work is a powerful asymmetry in the impacts of globalisation and global competition on the world's major industrial economies namely, record highs in the returns accruing to capital and record lows in the rewards going to labour.

So the experience of capitalist development reveals that the widening gulf of inequality arises from the great success of companies freed to operate anywhere in the globe. It derives from their ability to transfer to and expand production in countries where the cost of labour is lowest, and then distribute and sell their products in countries where prices are highest.

Extreme consumerism

The global web of profit-hunting corporations pours out a broadening torrent of commodities. But, without increasing numbers of consumers – whether prosperous or poor – to buy them, the whole process grinds to a halt. Everything and every service must be turned into a commodity sold for a profit. So every person must be turned into a consumer, wild with desires and determined to find the means to satisfy them.

Enter the persuaders, the marketing gurus alongside banks offering easy credit. Their job is to create insatiable cravings for things you never knew you needed, provide easy access, and equip you with ways of getting the money to buy them. Spiralling easy credit, combined with a big push on the underpinning ideology of private ownership, created a heady mix which drove property prices up and up.

A new home means a new fridge, washing machine, carpets, furniture, curtains... the list is endless. The revolution in technology spawned a blizzard of new products: phones, cameras, computers and infinite combinations sold under service contracts that ensured their replacement by the latest model on an at least annual basis, guaranteeing a tie-in to bandwidth use and a cash flow to the manufacturers under pressure to compete. Commodities for the billions struggling to survive on low incomes are cheapened to reduce or even eliminate their useful qualities, whilst retaining profitability. The need to constantly replace poor quality products designed not to last, is a key aspect of the consumer boom.

Pressure-selling of cheap, but unhealthy food has made many people simultaneously obese and malnourished. According to the World Health Organisation (WHO), obesity has reached epidemic proportions globally, with more than 1 billion adults overweight – at least 300 million of them clinically obese – and is a major contributor to the global burden of chronic disease and disability. Often coexisting in developing countries with under-nutrition, obesity is a complex condition, with serious social and psychological dimensions, affecting virtually all ages and socioeconomic groups.[7]

Another review for WHO found that children's advertising is dominated by food products, especially pre-sugared breakfast cereals, soft-drinks, confectionary and savoury snacks. "It is clear that children across the world are being exposed to an unhealthy diet through food promotion. Furthermore, globalisation and specifically the opening up of massive economies in India and China, mean that this marketing effort is set to increase. Food brands such as Coca-Cola and McDonald's can gain an almost iconic status in the conflation of development and the values of industrialized countries," says WHO.[8]

In the summer of 2002, during the depths of an extended financial and economic crisis affecting the whole of Latin America that saw Argentina's Gross National Product shrink by almost 20% in three years, Patricia Aguirre of Argentina's Ministry of Health and Social Action observed:

> The poor do not eat what they want, nor what they know that they should eat, but what they can get. Restrictions in access to food determine two simultaneous phenomena that are two sides of the same coin: poor people are malnourished because they do not have

enough to feed themselves, and they are obese because they eat poorly, with an important energy imbalance. The food they can afford is often cheap, industrialised, mass produced, and inexpensive.[9]

Personal debt

Meanwhile, consumers driven to despair by mounting debt in the UK are seeking support in record numbers. In September 2007, The Citizens Advice Bureau (CAB) said 1.7 million people sought debt counselling last year, up 20%. CAB is handling 6,600 debt enquiries a day. Those with problems paying credit card bills and other unsecured loans accounted for 40% of all enquiries. But CAB reported a "worrying" rise in the number of people struggling to meet day-to-day outgoings like phone bills. CAB said the figures illustrated how the consumer credit boom of the past decade – characterised by an easy availability of cheap credit and by people taking on more and more debt – had turned sour for many. "These figures are worrying evidence that while many have enjoyed the benefits of the credit boom, a large and growing number of people continue to pay the price," said David Harker, CAB's chief executive.

Bankruptcy-related enquiries rose 50% in 2006, while the number of people requiring help with their overdrafts rose 14%. Mortgage-related enquiries rose by 11%. Most disturbing of all, the CAB argued, was a 33% rise in the number of people struggling to pay their energy bills and a 25% rise in enquiries about council tax payments.

Resources wars

Sustaining growth means finding and extracting escalating quantities of raw materials as well as accessing increasing supplies of cheaper labour and widening markets. Corporations competing for resources are driven into conflict with each other, and with the governments and people of the countries in which the minerals and raw materials are located.

Africa is vastly rich in natural resources but the continent has paid a terrible price for this wealth. Horrific wars and conflicts in Angola, Sierra Leone, the Democratic Republic of Congo, Sudan and Liberia have been fuelled by fighting for control over diamonds, timber, gold, minerals and oil. Millions have been displaced and hundreds of thousands killed. Ibrahim Kamara, Sierra Leone's UN ambassador, said in July 2000: "We have always maintained that the conflict is not about ideology, tribal or regional difference... The root of the conflict is and remains diamonds, diamonds and diamonds."

As China's demands have grown, it too has been ready to back its trade deals and infrastructure investments with military assistance and arms, providing equipment to dictatorships in Burma, Zimbabwe and Sudan, assisting compliant governments to brutally quell popular opposition to the resources grab.

At the heart of the invasion of Iraq was the desire for access to that country's oil wealth and the drive to turn the country from a state to a market economy. In his memoirs *Age of Turbulence*, Alan Greenspan, former chairman of the Federal Reserve, admitted that "oil was one of the main reasons for waging war against Iraq". The writer Naomi Klein sheds some light on the other motivation for the shock and awe tactics used to destroy Iraq's ancient culture: opening it up as a new market for the global corporations. In *The Shock Doctrine: The Rise of Disaster Capitalism*, Klein writes:

> While the pickup trucks stuffed with loot were still being driven to buyers in Jordan, Syria and Iran, passing them in the opposite direction were convoys of flatbeds piled high with Chinese TVs, Hollywood DVDs and Jordanian satellite dishes, ready to be unloaded on the sidewalks of Baghdad's Karada district. Just as one culture was being burned and stripped for parts, another was pouring in, pre-packaged, to replace it. One of the US businesses ready and waiting to be the gateway to this experiment in frontier capitalism was New Bridge Strategies, started by Joe Allbaugh, Bush's ex-head of Fema [Federal Emergency Management Agency]. It promised to use its top-level political connections to help US multinationals land a piece of the action in Iraq. 'Getting the rights to distribute Procter & Gamble products would be a gold mine,' one of the company's partners enthused. 'One well-stocked 7-Eleven could knock out 30 Iraqi stores; a Wal-Mart could take over the country.'[10]

The number of US troops in Iraq is now at a peak of 168,000; but they rely on an even bigger army of 180,000 contractors, employed by more than two dozen private companies. Many of these people do the cooking and laundry. But about a quarter of them are fighters, doing the jobs traditionally done by soldiers. They protect US military operations and have guarded high-ranking officials, journalists, visiting foreign officials and thousands of construction projects.

Blackwater, which has earned nearly $1bn from the American government, is notoriously trigger-happy, opening fire first in 163 out of 195 shooting incidents since 2005, according to a report by Congress. On 16 September 2007, Blackwater guards opened fire in a crowded Baghdad square and killed as many as 17 people and wounded 24.

A market state

Financier George Soros hoped that the collapse of the Soviet Union would lead to what he calls "open societies". But by 2000 he was already warning:

> Perhaps the greatest threat to freedom and democracy in the world today comes from the formation of unholy alliances between government and business. This is not a new phenomenon. It used to be called fascism...The outward appearances of the democratic process are preserved, but the powers of the state are diverted to the benefit of private interests.

This ever-closer merging of the capitalist state, politics and economics is one of the most significant consequences of globalisation. We have witnessed the transition from a welfare to a competition or market state in parallel with the dramatic changes to the structure of the global economy. Now the state sees its role as directly promoting the market economy, while handing over decision-making to non-elected bodies like the WTO.

Whole areas of public services and industries are privatised. Public projects like schools and hospitals are themselves conditional on private finance and contracts that guarantee fantastic returns at no risk. The market now penetrates every area of what was the welfare state, including housing, health, dentistry, public transport and legal aid.

At the same time, a mounting authoritarianism, introduced under the cloak of the "war on terror", has swept away many democratic rights.

Representative government is reduced to a sham, helping to create an historic crisis of legitimacy of the current state system of rule in Britain and elsewhere.

New Labour especially champions the ideology of global capitalism. Gordon Brown told financiers just before becoming prime minister that history would record that the government had helped put to work "that set of qualities that is needed for global success". According to Brown, these were "openness to the world and global reach", being "pioneers of free trade", having "a deep and abiding belief in open markets" as well as "flexibility and adaptability to change". Within a few weeks, the same government was bailing out Northern Rock!

Many of the state's activities are directed towards the globalisation project. Take education. In the same speech, Brown told the City fat cats: "Only with investment in education can open markets, free trade and flexibility succeed... If we can show people that by equipping themselves for the future they can be the winners not losers in globalisation... then people will welcome open, flexible, free trade and pro-competition economies as an emancipating force."

The practical result of the transition to a market, competition state is that notions that capitalism can be reformed through parliamentary activity are inconceivable. Labour, which was a party based on class compromise and wringing some concessions from the ruling classes, is now New Labour – the party of choice for the global élites operating in Britain, at least for the time being.

References

1. Intergovernmental Panel on Climate Change http://www.ipcc.ch/index.html

2. *Climate Change 2007: The Physical Science Basis, Summary for Policymakers,* Intergovernmental Panel on Climate Change, http://www.ipcc.ch/SPM2feb07.pdf

3. Stern Review http://www.hm-treasury.gov.uk/independent_reviews/stern_review_ economics_climate_change/sternreview_index.cfm

4. http://uk.reuters.com/article/environmentNews/idUKSYD21253520070829

5. Pollution From Chinese Coal Casts a Global Shadow, *New York Times,* 11 June 2006 http://www.nytimes.com/2006/06/11/business/worldbusiness/11chinacoal.html?ex=130767 8400en=e9ac1f6255a24fd8ei=5088partner=rssnytemc=rss

6. *The World Distribution of Household Wealth,* World Institute for Development Economics Research of the United Nations University (UNU-WIDER) 5 December 2006, http://www.mindfully.org/WTO/2006/Household-Wealth-Gap5dec06.htm

7. *Global Strategy on Diet, Physical Activity and Health* http://www.who.int/dietphysicalactivity/publications/facts/obesity/en/

8. *The Extent, Nature and Effects of Food Promotion to Children: A Review of the Evidence* Technical Paper prepared for the World Health Organization, Gerard Hastings, Laura McDermott, Kathryn Angus, Martine Stead and Stephen Thomson, Institute for Social Marketing, University of Stirling & The Open University, United Kingdom July 2006

9. The faces of poverty: Malnourished, hungry, and obese? *Obesity* 26 August 2002 http://www.obgyn.net/newsheadlines/headline_medical_news-Obesity-20020826-7.asp

10. Naomi Klein, *The Shock Doctrine: The Rise of Disaster Capitalism,* Allen Lane 2007

4

A leopard cannot change its spots

Many groups, as well as distinguished individuals, appalled in one way or another by what global capitalism has done to the planet, believe that the solution lies in a mixture of regulation, state intervention, new global governance and changes to the way corporations operate.

In essence, they argue that if only we could tame the beast, draw the sting from transnational corporations and financial institutions, the world would be a better place. We would then have a kinder, gentler globalisation that would benefit all of human kind.

Advocates of this capitalism with a human face include the leading economics professor Joseph Stiglitz, who once advised the World Bank, pressure groups such as the World Development Movement (WDM), Greenpeace, the Campaign Against Climate Change and Oxfam, as well as the International Labour Organisation (ILO). In a major 2004 report, the ILO calls for a "fair globalisation" to create "opportunities for all" and says: "We judge that the problems we have identified are not due to globalisation as such but to deficiencies in its **governance**." [emphasis added] In 190 pages of text, analysis and graphs, the ILO unbelievably fails to apply the term capitalism even once to the study of globalisation and its social impact.

The WDM campaigns against what it identifies as "the root causes of poverty" and its website adds: "We lobby decision-makers to stop policies that hurt the world's poor... We mobilise consumers, shareholders and governments to hold multinational companies accountable for abuses of power. We are lobbying for **reform** of the World Trade Organisation (WTO)." [emphasis added]

The financier-philanthropist George Soros, one of the world's richest men, also wants to rescue capitalist globalisation from itself. Ironically, it was speculation against sterling by Soros' Quantum Fund that in 1992 was an early indicator of the rise and rise of financial corporations with powers beyond those commanded by governments. In *George Soros on Globalisation*, he sketches out specific proposals to solve the systemic flaws of international capitalism that he cited in his previous book, *The Crisis of Global Capitalism*. The present system, Soros believes, creates an "unfair playing field", with the United States and other developed countries managing the system at the expense of developing countries. The heart of the book includes concrete proposals for reforming international institutions, reducing the instability of markets, and fighting world poverty. Before completing the book, Soros convened a special conference, of eminent international scholars.

The most eminent scholar present was Stiglitz. He is a Nobel economics laureate and professor of economics at Columbia University and one of the world's foremost critics of globalisation. After leaving the World Bank, where he was chief economist and senior vice-president, Stiglitz wrote *Globalization and its Discontents*, which exposes the devastation wrought by the International Monetary Fund's "structural adjustment" programmes in Asia and Russia. His latest book is *Making Globalisation Work* where he outlines "practical ways" in which the functioning of the international political economy could be improved. He argues against the way globalisation "has been managed". Stiglitz advocates more democracy – but only in the realms of a change in the voting structures of the IMF and World Bank and their representation. Far from rejecting market mechanisms, his aim is to make markets work. Take his case against intellectual-property rights. Stiglitz argues that patents hold knowledge hostage and therefore obstruct the proper working of market forces. Stiglitz lavishes praise on the "benefits" brought to the global economy by transnational corporations.

The Third World Network (TWN) campaigns for a better deal for developing countries and is an influential NGO. Director Martin Khor even manages to get invitations to the World Economic Forum at Davos. In one presentation, he told the assembled corporate chief executives: "Until the **reforms** to the system and to the substance of the WTO take place, the organisation's credibility will remain low." [emphasis added] As is well documented, the WTO moves in near secrecy. Most, if not all, of its key decisions are worked out in informal meetings. Reforming the WTO is a tall order, putting it mildly. As the TWN itself admits on its website:

> Where these meetings took place, when, and who attended, as well as the positions taken by the various countries, are not made known. When these small informal groups work out decisions among themselves, they are taken before the formal meetings, and made into decisions. Most times, the 'major countries' (the largest developed countries) get the decisions they want. A few big countries are also able to veto the issues or decisions they do not want even if the vast majority of countries agree to them. In fact, often, when the US and the EC [European Commission] do not want an issue to be raised, it does not even come before the formal sessions.

Then there are advocates of a tax on global currency transactions. Named after the economist James Tobin, such a tax is intended to put a penalty on short-term speculation in currencies and was first put forward after the break-up of Bretton Woods in 1971. The idea lay dormant for more than 20 years. Then in 1997 Ignacio Ramonet, editor of *Le Monde Diplomatique*, proposed an association for the introduction of this tax, which was named ATTAC (Association for the Taxation of financial Transactions for the Aid of Citizens). The idea is to persuade governments to levy the tax as a way of curbing speculation while raising large amounts of revenue for socially-useful projects.

Others concentrate on ways to limit growth, which is viewed as the most destructive side of capitalism. The New Economics Foundation (NEF) argues that it "isn't growth so much as the quality of our lives that counts". It proposes to reformulate "sustainable objectives" and other measures in order to redefine what constitutes progress as an alternative to using economic growth as a yardstick. The corporations would then have to be persuaded to adopt this new criteria. Clive Hamilton, in his *Visions of the Future – the post-growth society*, writes:

> Growth not only fails to make people contented; it also destroys many of the things that do. Growth fosters empty consumerism, degrades the natural environment, weakens social cohesion and corrodes character.

While what both the NEF and Hamilton say is correct, they nevertheless give growth an almost autonomous power and significance, separate from capitalism itself. In fact, as we have shown, the need for continuous growth is built into the heart of the capitalist system and is inextricably linked to the tendency of the rate of profit to fall as productivity advances.

The campaign group Simpol promotes Simultaneous Policy (SP), "which aims to deliver social justice around the world, resolve global problems like environmental destruction and regulate the economic power of international capital for the good of all". Simpol says it seeks solutions to problems that individual national governments cannot resolve by acting alone, adding: "This is because the problems transcend national boundaries, and because the global competitive system means that any government that acted alone to try and resolve such problems could effectively make its country uncompetitive."

You could not disagree with these sentiments but the way forward that Simpol proposes is the height of idealism. The group aims to achieve these objectives by "encouraging ordinary people around the world to oblige their political representatives and governments to move toward co-ordinated international resolution of global issues for the good of all". Simultaneous implementation of such policies would ensure that no country became uncompetitive in adopting the new approach. This touching faith in capitalist democracy and the seeming capacity of the system to reform itself is totally misplaced.

Others go much further. The International Forum on Globalisation (IFG) rejects the idea of reforming the existing system of global capitalist governance. Instead, in *Economic Alternatives to Globalisation* the IFG advocates some principles for building sustainable societies which would lead to greater democracy. These include new institutions of "global governance" to replace the World Bank, the IMF and the

WTO. The idea is that a reshaped United Nations would lead the discussion and changes that the IFG advocates.

Reality check

All these proposals, whatever their source or form, are a reaction to the consequences of corporate-driven globalisation outlined in the previous chapter. Because they ignore – or in many instances actually accept – the fundamental premises of capitalist economy, their chances of success are slim to non-existent.

Domestic and international regulation of money supply through a gold or silver standard has a chequered history. In the last quarter of the 19th century, most capitalist states adopted the gold standard for international trade. They were joined by the United States in 1900. But capitalism's inner movement drove it beyond the gold standard's restrictions. This took the form of colonial conquest and imperialism, which were the driving forces for the mass slaughter of World War I. Attempts to revive the gold standard after the war floundered amid economic crisis and Britain pulled out in 1931.

After World War II, a new system of fixed currencies and controls on speculative capital outflows was set up. The aim was to direct capital into industry and trade. But the system lasted less than 30 years, collapsing in 1971 when the US government severed the link between gold and the dollar.

In virtually all countries, formerly state-owned industries and utilities have been privatised as part of the deregulation process. As we have shown, the deregulation of currency markets and capital flows has created an entirely new global financial system which is subject to the minimum of controls. Central banks and regulators in many cases have no inkling as to what is taking place in financial markets.

Deregulation is an absolute requirement of corporate-driven globalisation and lies at the heart of the system. The chief executive officer of the hi-tech NASDAQ exchange Robert Greifeld told Boston businessmen in September 2006: "The world has followed our lead. [Stock] exchanges have been globalised and their investor base has been globalised." Greifeld added that "as we go to globalisation of markets" he was confident of seeing "a global race to the bottom with respect to regulation". A survey for the New York Stock Exchange of top CEOs in

September 2007 found – surprise, surprise – that 89% would consider the streamlining of the US regulatory system and the easing of certain governance rules and regulations as positive moves.

In Britain, New Labour has created the Department for Business, Enterprise and Regulatory Reform and there is even a Better Regulation Executive which is "tasked by the Prime Minister with cutting red tape so that businesses can be more productive and public services more efficient, by legislating only where necessary and deregulating and simplifying existing legislation wherever possible".

Proposals for greater regulation also greatly over-estimate the capacity of governments to act under globalisation. For example, the current crisis in the financial markets reveals how little influence governments and central banks have. Commenting on the credit crunch, Anthony Hilton, business editor of the London *Evening Standard*, pointed out:

> How do you constrain an industry that is essentially intangible? As big a shock as any coming crash might be the realisation that there are no longer any easy regulatory answers. We might instead just have to get used to a world where the British economy is little more than a hedge fund with a gigantic one-way bet on financial services. (7 August 2007)

As far as the Bank of England is concerned, Hilton was even more scathing, suggesting that it looks "increasingly as if it is in office but not in power". Hilton added:

> It and the other central banks around the world, including the most powerful, the Federal Reserve bank in Washington, are having to come to terms with the fact that these days the influence lies elsewhere, in the hands of the investment banks and their similarly driven colleagues in the world financial centres. They have in effect hijacked the world financial system and with it the global economy... Meanwhile, Bank of England Governor Mervyn King looks ever more like one of those toddlers to be seen in the model cars outside supermarkets, turning the wheel like a maniac but in fact playing with controls that are not connected to anything.

Emerging economies like China and India have amassed vast dollar holdings and, at the same time, are outside of the IMF structures. This limits even further the capacity of global agencies to influence the course of financial crises.

Broken free

The very essence of corporate-driven globalisation is that it has largely broken free from nation-state constraints and transcends borders in its operations. Even if states wanted to regulate the activities of the global market, they have neither the incentive nor the capacity to do so. They are in the main so tied to corporate interests that any attempt to impose burdensome regulations will simply lead to business and finance moving elsewhere. It's that "global race to the bottom" again.

Secondly, it is inconceivable that capitalist nation states throughout the world could summon up the political will to even attempt such a project. Their failure to act in a concerted way to deal with climate change is evidence of their inablity to act for the benefit of humanity as a whole, rather than the narrow interests of the corporations. In other words, the advocates of regulation are faced with the challenge of reversing an unfolding process, of turning the clock of economic and political history backwards four decades. Clearly, this is an impossible task. Moreover, it ignores the fact that governments like New Labour are facilitators for the needs of the corporations and the global market economy.

In any case, the way institutions created by global capitalism such as the WTO operate, resembles the corporate interests they serve. The WTO operates on a one country, one vote system, but actual votes have never been taken. Decision making is generally by consensus, and relative market size is the primary source of bargaining power. Those who advocate reform also imply that democracy and capitalism are compatible, and that governments will always have to respond to the popular will.

When capitalism plunges into crisis, the democratic façade can be stripped away in rapid order, as history has demonstrated over and over again. Fascism in Germany, Italy and Spain was not the result of megalomanic leaders, human nature or racist nations but the ultimate logic of a system no longer able to rule through democratic channels.

There are even more fundamental reasons than these why capitalism cannot change its spots. As we have shown, the heart of the system is the production of commodities for profit. What this produces in practice is an irrational and destructive economic system that is to a large extent beyond control. When viewed as a totalising system, rather than a series of discrete parts, capitalism displays an independent logic of development and change that defies control and regulation except in the most limited sense.

Neither is capitalist globalisation simply a set of ideas and beliefs sometimes labelled, rather euphemistically and confusingly, as "neo-liberalism". It has an objective existence and dynamic, which is primary to its ideological expression. The profit motive is not an idea – it is an imperative by which capitalism lives or dies.

The profit drive carries with it the inescapable goals of relentless growth, control of people and command over resources rather than the needs of individuals, communities or the environment. Because profits and shareholder value must grow year on year, there is a phenomenal waste of raw materials and energy resources. In the effort to avoid costs, capitalism pollutes the air, the water, and the soil. The result is an acceleration of climate change.

Global capitalism operates across continents and has created an international division of labour. Yet despite its highly socialised character, the system is founded on private ownership of the means of production and the alienation of the workforce from the fruits of their labour. Capitalism produces commodities for profit for markets instead of need, and so compels consumers to buy what they do not necessarily need or want, or cannot in reality afford, through extensive credit and debt arrangements. Capitalism talks about peace yet maintains a military-industrial complex complete with vast armies directed at developing countries and domestic populations alike. Capitalism is in sum an alienating, irrational system that poses a danger to the future of humanity.

The harsh reality is that in order to reform the economic system, to make it serve the needs of ordinary people, a revolutionary transformation of social relations is required. The route to achieving this change is explored in the next chapter.

5

Composting capitalism

The period of unprecedented economic growth and technological revolution of the past three decades has provided the means for satisfying the material needs of humanity; yet capitalist society denies them to most people on the planet.

Productive capacity, skills and resources exist that could meet every individual's needs. But more than one billion people have no safe water to drink. More than one billion are forced to live in slums. Hundreds of millions throughout the world are without a livelihood while workers in the major countries are drowning in debt, face intensive exploitation and job insecurity.

The unfolding global recession shows that the capitalist, profit-led system that grew to dominate the world over three and a half centuries is now devouring itself and is unsustainable. Reduce, reuse and recycle cannot co-exist with the insistent drumbeat of consumption needed to maintain capitalist production. The mounting consequences of climate change, financial and economic disorder and war have led us to a crucial moment for the planet and its inhabitants. Humanity has arrived at an historical crossroads where we face key decisions. Our aim must be to extend the gains and advances that capitalism provides for a minority to all people in all countries through the development of a global society based on co-operation, co-ownership and sustainability.

We put forward the following principles as a way to act globally by starting locally:

- ownership of production facilities of the major corporations and of land and water through a variety of forms of co-ownership
- democratic control and self-management of economic and financial resources, including public services
- productive capacity shifted towards satisfying need rather than generating profit
- ecologically sustainable production and distribution
- encouraging and supporting small-scale enterprises, creative workers and farmers to work sustainably
- favouring local production for local needs
- facilitating the development of the "thinking market".

The present political system cannot deliver the changes that are required through regulation, taxation or new laws. It has, after all, facilitated the takeover by the TNCs and handed vast powers to unelected bodies like the World Trade Organisation and the European Commission. Governments and states have become voluntary warders patrolling the global economy on behalf of the corporations. They have promoted deregulation and privatisation, imposing competition in the public sector and undermining workplace rights. Britain and the United States have launched disastrous and illegal wars in Iraq and Afghanistan and declared that only market "solutions" that favour the global capitalist economy are acceptable in the face of climate chaos.

To break the deadlock, we need to move on in history, both economically and politically. The capitalist period that stretches back little more than 200 years has outlived its usefulness and purpose. The same holds true for the parliamentary political system. The market state's priorities are the endless and futile "war on terror" and the upholding of the economic and political status quo.

A World to Win believes that in order to achieve our goals we must challenge the political and moral support for capitalism as the organising premise of society. As we have demonstrated, there are no solutions to the planetary crisis through protest, pressure, regulation or the feeble and powerless parliamentary political system.

To create the conditions for sustainable change, nothing short of a revolutionary transformation of the state system that maintains capitalism in power is needed. In the place of the existing discredited, undemocratic, unaccountable political system, we have to develop new decentralised, networked forms of democratic government to work out equitable solutions for all.

A rapidly increasing number of people are dissatisfied with the status quo and are eager for change. They are represented in a diverse array of campaigns and initiatives, consumer action groups, climate camps, anti-war and anti-poverty campaigns. Tens of thousands of trade unionists like postal workers have opposed privatisation and the worsening of their conditions in the name of "competition" and "market forces".

Transition Town groups are forming in many towns and cities, villages and localities to anticipate and work out solutions to the issues arising from the twin problems of the imminent reduction of oil production as it reaches its peak, and the urgent need to reduce carbon emissions to limit global warming. Fair trade organisations work primarily with small businesses, democratically-run associations, and/or co-operatives which bring significant benefits to workers and their communities. Co-operatives and producer associations provide a healthy alternative to large-scale manufacturing and sweatshops conditions.

These movements and the millions who will join them tomorrow as capitalism proves incapable of solving any of the pressing problems facing humanity, can and must become the force for revolutionary economic and political change.

The dividing line is clear. Jonathon Porritt, the eminent environmental activist and government adviser,[1] simply wants a different form of capitalism and says:

> Against this backdrop of worsening inequality, collapsing eco-systems, negative climate change, unchecked self-interest, obscene spending on arms and war, the protection of world leaders of the inconceivably rich minority, and the failure of globalisation to deliver its promise to the world's poorest countries, I see an ideal opportunity for the ethos of the Co-operative Movement to inform and inspire a very different kind of globalisation, one which puts people first, prosperity and planet next, and profits after that. The truth of it is that our **particular model of capitalism** today is stuffed! [emphasis added]

It's inconceivable that it could deliver the kind of equitable, sustainable society that nine billion people will be hoping to live in by 2050. However, capitalism is – quite literally – the only economic game in town. So what we have to create (ideally over the next ten years) is a **different kind of capitalism** – and what better inspiration is there for that kind of transformation than the principles and practices of the co-operative movement. Is there any other global movement that has a better claim to such a role? [emphasis added]

What we propose instead is a different kind of society altogether. New forms of co-ownership of major production and financial resources would be enshrined in law in place of the private ownership for profit of the corporations, banks and investment firms. These would adapt and develop the principles of the co-operative movement.

Co-ownership

By banding together, workers are able to access credit, reduce raw material costs and establish more just prices for their products. Workers earn a greater return on their labour, and profits are distributed more equitably. Profits are also often reinvested in community projects, such as health clinics, child care, education and training.

Workers practice important leadership and organising skills, enabling self-reliant grassroots-driven development. Safe and healthy working

---

Ownership stake

Although so far constrained by the need to coexist in a capitalist economy, the evidence is that people who co-own the companies they work in and collaborate in decision-making, are happier, more productive, more committed, more satisfied, and that the businesses they work in are not only more successful economically, but are better liked by customers.

The Employee Ownership Association reports that firms where staff have a big ownership stake and a say in decisions are more productive because employees feel happier at work. John Lewis and Waitrose, both parts of the employee-owned John Lewis Partnership, recently topped a survey of the nation's favourite shops. [2] According to Barry Cooke, boss of co-owned architects Make: "People who feel good about themselves and their job create a better product – it is as simple as that."

conditions are maintained and producers gain greater control and decision-making power over the use of their resources.

Many organisations have grown up as a defence against the destructive demands and impact of unsustainable methods of profit-led competitive production. These form the basis of transforming private ownership into

What the Suma co-op say about themselves

Ah, the magic 'C' word. We don't really like to blow our own trumpet here at Suma, but we do like to think that being a workers' cooperative is one of the fundamental keys to our success. So what's it all about? Unlike most UK companies, Suma operates a truly democratic system of management that isn't bound by the conventional notions of hierarchy that often hinder progress and stand in the way of fairness. While we do use an elected Management Committee to implement decisions and business plans, the decisions themselves are made at regular General Meetings with the consent of every cooperative member – there's no chief executive, no managing director and no company chairman. In practice, this means that our day-to-day work is carried out by self-managing teams of employees who are all paid the same wage, and who all enjoy an equal voice and an equal stake in the success of the business.

Another key feature of our structure and working practice is multi-skilling. At Suma we encourage members to get involved in more than one area of business, so individuals will always perform more than one role within the cooperative. This helps to broaden our skills base and give every member an invaluable insight into the bigger picture. It also helps us to play to each member's various different strengths while enabling us to think 'outside the box' when it comes to creativity and problem solving. And as for job satisfaction and staff morale – just ask yourself when was the last time you heard someone complain that their job involved too much variety? It is the spice of life, after all.

This all sounds great, but does it work? In a word, yes. Here in the UK we're often sceptical about workers' co-operatives, but that's largely because of our more conventional business culture and the fact that the vast majority of UK companies are purely profit-driven. Workers' co-operatives are far more common in many advanced European countries and developing world economies. Of course it's not all plain sailing, but if you look at Suma's growth over its 30-year history, we think you'll agree that we must be doing something right.

Suma is the UK's largest independent wholefood wholesaler-distributor
www.suma.co.uk

co-operative, community-driven forms of ownership and control. The co-operative movement is far from new, having developed alongside the trade union movement. It began as a response to the impact of the 19th century industrial revolution as the increasing mechanisation of the economy transformed society and threatened the livelihoods of many workers. Its principles call for voluntary and open membership, democratic member control, member economic participation, autonomy and independence, education, training, and information, co-operation among co-operatives and concern for community.

▶ The International Co-operative Alliance has 221 member organisations from 86 countries active in all sectors of the economy. Together these co-operatives represent more than 800 million individuals worldwide. They include workers' co-operatives, consumer co-operatives and agricultural co-operatives

▶ The World Council of Credit Unions (WOCCU) which represents the worldwide movement has members and affiliates in 92 countries around the world. Members include regional and national credit union associations, co-operative associations, and business service organisations. Together, they represent more than 42,616 credit unions serving 157 million members

▶ altogether more than one billion people worldwide are directly involved in co-operatives

▶ co-operatives provide over 100 million jobs around the world, 20% more than transnational enterprises.

Even within capitalist state structures, large areas of public life are still run largely on a not-for-profit basis. These include the National Health Service, education and local authority services. Many of the serious

Open source

Internet-based voluntary open source software collaborations produced Linux and Apache, the not-for-profit foundations of the rapidly-evolving Web. New models of social networking together with digital media are forcing a rethink of intellectual copyright and revolutionising design, production and distribution of music, movies, aircraft, automobiles and even gold prospecting. This is the technological basis for a new type of society.

problems of the NHS are due to its cannibalisation by private interests, PFI, and milking by the pharmaceutical giants. Popular resistance to their full privatisation not only shows that they could work perfectly well without the profit motive but that support for co-operative forms of working is widespread.

Together with the remaining state enterprises, co-operatively owned, not-for-profit enterprises can form the basis of a new approach to economic life. They could inspire a movement whose aim is the transfer of ownership of the TNCs into community control and self-management.

Self-management

The principles of self-management practised in the co-operative movement can easily be applied to the operations of major global enterprises taken into co-ownership. Take the example of food. Under self-management, all the existing enterprises – supermarkets, distribution facilities, processing plants, food producers and farmers – will co-operate in interdependent, self-managed networks.

Each separate enterprise would contract with purchase/supply partners. Prices will be determined by the costs of production, taking into account sustainable methods of agriculture and processing, the livelihoods of those involved in production, distribution and retailing and the cost of recycling or safely disposing of any waste. Each enterprise will be run by an elected workers' council with access to a wide range of expert, financial, technical and scientific advice. The responsibilities of those involved in self-management could include:

▶ working locally with representatives of consumer, hospitals, schools, social services and other large users to ensure local needs are identified and met
▶ taking advice from experts in the fields of nutrition, food economics and safety
▶ identifying with consumers what new products can be developed and supplied to meet both local and national needs
▶ ensuring that food hygiene, safety and nutritional qualities meet agreed standards
▶ identifying what can be produced locally and what needs to be acquired from elsewhere

- ▶ formulating proposals on their own working conditions, hours and salaries
- ▶ ensuring that revenues generated from these activities are accounted for and that contractual obligations in the supply chain are fulfilled
- ▶ producing a democratically-arrived at plan for food supply in the short, medium and long-term for submission to local representative bodies.

Many of these tasks are already carried out in a haphazard and often unco-ordinated way within capitalist society by salaried workers. The aim here is to set them within a new framework of social responsibility and accountability. This approach to self-management and democratic planning could become a model for all branches of industry and services.

Liberating capitalism from itself

We are not, however, proposing to do away with all the structures of global corporations. Global networks, global systems for production and distribution and a global division of labour are advances for human society, though at present they serve profit-motivated corporate requirements.

Many of the component parts of the system can be reused or recycled. We need to preserve these advances in a new global economy oriented towards the satisfaction of needs. Capitalism can and should be composted. Capitalism has developed an array of potentially useful methods and technologies. Once liberated from the straitjacket of profit and private ownership, these will form the basis of the sustainable society of the future. They include:

- ▶ a globally interconnected communications infrastructure
- ▶ scientific systems of management
- ▶ highly-skilled workforces in many countries
- ▶ integrated methods of supply, production and distribution
- ▶ the continuing scientific and technological revolution
- ▶ a global financial system.

Concentrated in only a few advanced countries they benefit a small percentage of the world's population. A new democratic society serving the needs of the majority will ensure that the beneficial results of capitalist production are made available to all in a fully integrated, socialised system of production and distribution.

Communications infrastructure

In an equitable society focussed on need, the benefits of the computing and communications revolution will be made universally available. A global spiders' web of optical fibre and satellites, enhanced with mobile telephony, personal wireless devices, and the continuously increasing speed and power of networked computer systems will serve humanity. A new generation of the Internet will draw the wealth of data, information and knowledge management systems into an interconnected layer of intelligence which will be deployed to enhance co-operation.

Through free and open access to intellectual products, every individual could create boundless opportunities for self-development. Scarce, specialist expertise can be shared across the globe. Remotely-controlled surgery and other aspects of telemedicine already open pathways to the future. In a fully-integrated network using multipoint tele- and video-conferencing, the majority can become participants in policy-making, planning and decision-making. In this way, participative democracy will extend far beyond the primitive forms of registering votes electronically.

When energy production and transportation are socially owned, new generations of planes, high, medium and low speed trains, trams and hybrid vehicles using low and no carbon fuel systems (liquid petroleum gas, electric, solar, hydrogen) will be drawn together into an integrated and sustainable transport system.

Radio frequency and biometric identification devices help track any tagged object as it moves. Information can be available instantly on any object or process on the planet. Repressive governments eye these technologies as means of social control, using ID cards and electronically-tagged irremovable bracelets or anklets as a prison without walls. In a democratic society bent on satisfying the needs of the majority, the emphasis will be on control of objects not people.

Scientific systems of management

Transnational and global corporations were made possible by scientific approaches to management. They have eliminated many layers of management and hierarchies. To survive the technological revolution, all organisations have to learn how to manage change, whilst retaining their identity and sense of purpose. They use and develop techniques which will prove invaluable in the social revolution, constructing and operating a new, democratically-controlled economy.

Emerging social systems will develop from, and be based upon dynamic, fluid, inter-related, interdependent networks of autonomous self-organising, self-reorganising, self-managed structures/units. These will be linked by thousands of connections into a new continuously evolving whole, but sharing a collective vision and purpose and contributing to the well-being of all.

Highly-skilled workforces

The technological revolution demands highly developed, IT-literate workforces, with individuals able to move easily from job to job as production methods change, entire industries disappear and new ones arise. Flexible workplace practices, such as team work and multi-skilling, require more highly skilled and better educated workforces. In planned production, reduced hours can be shared to everyone's benefit, rather than intensifying exploitation while unemployment soars. Under capitalism, these attributes are distorted by profit and alienate workers who do not own the end product and have no control over how it is produced or distributed. In co-owned, self-managed enterprises change can be – and is – managed to their benefit.

Many TNCs are giant holding companies characterised by a diverse range of products, highly responsive supply chain management, globally-distributed planned production systems, automated production and a broad range of marketing techniques. Many of these characteristics will be carried forward into new systems organised around the principles of sustainability, local sourcing and local distribution.

Scientific and technological revolution

The immediate tasks are to clear up the mess resulting from the old capitalist system of production. A new sense of purpose will replace profit as the determinant of the direction and pace of technological innovation. Knowledge will advance in leaps and bounds as the commercialisation of intellectual property rights is ended. New technologies will be subject to rigorous testing, and the risks of premature introduction assessed against their contribution to improving the well-being of the population and of ecosystems.

Early action on energy conservation and sustainable energy systems will supersede the destructive thirst for oil. Cleaning up and recycling emissions from coal and gas-fired power stations are high priority, as are safe solutions for decommissioning nuclear installations and disposing of waste. Rapid progress is needed to find and deploy antidotes for the heavy metals and other pollutants such as PCBs and dioxins which have been dumped in lakes, rivers and seas for decades.

Constructive use of technology will encourage areas such as synthetic biology, currently at the stage of experiment and demonstration. Living machines will help to dispose of nuclear waste, biological and chemical weapons and to fabricate anti-malarial drugs cheaply. Competitive pressure for early implementation of new drugs and gene-based technologies will be replaced by strict application of the precautionary principle – first do no harm.

The benefits of genetic counselling and gene therapy in reducing the impact of inherited diseases are already beginning to be realised. As more knowledge of the interaction between external and internal factors becomes available, the relative importance of social, preventative action and individual healthcare interventions will become clearer and can be acted upon. When monopoly profits on herbicides such as glyphosate are removed from the equation, the marketing hype surrounding the contribution of new seeds to eliminating world hunger will subside and objective assessment will prevail.

As research into the applications of nano- and bio-technologies bears new fruit, such as self-constructing and self-repairing machines, new and even more spectacular leaps in the power, speed and availability of computing are coming on stream. A dialectic of development, with each branch of science feeding the other, will deliver unimaginable contributions to the collective future of humanity when the new social paradigm comes into play.

A global financial system

In the 1990s, the computing and communications revolution paved the way for the globalisation of financial markets. With the elimination of private equity shareholding, and the abolition of speculation on the money markets, the techniques developed by global capitalism can be used to clear payments between enterprises within and between countries. Accounting systems can be used and further developed to be open to public scrutiny. The dream of a moneyless society can become a reality.

No-one should lose their home as a consequence of the failing system which exists to extract profit from dependence on the essential need for a place to live. All banks and former building societies involved in the mortgage business should be turned over to mutual status. The mortgages they hold will have to be cancelled, and new arrangements agreed and established through democratic debate. The millions of properties they hold as collateral against loans should be taken over by not-for-profit housing bodies.

The thinking market

In today's manufacturing process, advanced systems track progress through the various stages of production, assembly and delivery. Many companies now make stage-by-stage progress on orders available to customers on their websites, as do parcel collection and delivery companies. Though developed to sustain profits through increased productivity, they can be re-engineered to identify and address need. Advanced methods of needs analysis and market research, incorporating predictive demography, will inform strategic, long-term planning. The results will consist of guidelines for building sustainable production and distribution capacity worldwide.

Methods of measuring consumption can be developed, building on the most sophisticated existing loyalty card and market information databases. These will be deployed to ensure that production and distribution of goods respond to individual wants, within the limits that have been agreed collectively.

Producing on demand to satisfy individual taste has already become normal in some industries. Many cars and computers are assembled only when an order has been placed. While satisfying needs already agreed, the thinking market will expand to respond to many more individual expressions of want.

Distribution of wealth

The distribution of profits to shareholders – the current private owners of capital – will cease. Stock, currency and other markets for speculation will be closed. The wealth generated by workers realised from sales of their products will be distributed according to the following principles:

- ► a part will be paid to the workers in the enterprise. An individual's income from employment will be set in relation to the basic living wage, supplemented by skill and performance-related amounts
- ► a part will be retained for reinvestment in, and further development of the organisation
- ► the value generated by an organisation, over and above the wages paid to workers, and the amounts retained for reinvestment, will be divided amongst the Social Needs Funds
- ► these funds will support education and research; health and social care; recreation and the arts; infrastructure development including energy, communications and transport; pensions, and incomes for those unable to work through disability or illness
- ► the proportion of the social surplus allocated to each of the various Social Needs Funds will be determined through planning rounds controlled by the democratic process.

The future

In replacing the failing capitalist system of production we seek to:

- ► ensure the majority have access to the benefits currently only available to the few
- ► ensure survival of the planet, ecosystems and humanity
- ► create a society based on co-operation, satisfying need and not profit
- ► release the potential of automation, reducing working hours substantially
- ► overcome alienation of people from their work, what is produced and society as a whole
- ► use the abundance of products to alleviate poverty and need world-wide
- ► allow and enable people to fulfil their potential and aspirations
- ► make health and well-being the single dominant social objective for the world's population.

The burden of debt repayment imposed on the people of the poor countries as the price of forced entry into the world market will be cancelled. The IMF, World Bank and WTO will top the list for replacement with new institutions directly accountable to a global Assembly. These will take measures to ensure that incomes and the standard of living are progressively equalised around the world.

Society can then move forward decisively to the time when everyone in each country can live in the fullest sense according to their needs.

References

1. *The Co-operative* membership magazine (Autumn 2007)

2. *Which?* Customer satisfaction survey, February 2007

The future depends on you

A House of Cards is a call for an alternative to profit-driven corporate power and undemocratic political rule. Building support for **A World to Win** is vital if we are to inspire people to make the kind of revolutionary change outlined in the pages of this booklet.

A World to Win as an organisation believes that the existing state is undemocratic, unrepresentative and dominated by corporate interests.

A World to Win campaigns for a transfer of political and economic power to the working majority in society and for the reorganisation of the economy along co-operative, not-for-profit, self-management lines.

A World to Win is based on a group structure, reflecting priorities and interests decided by all members. We strive to create a networked, non-hierarchical, interactive organisation. AWTW emphasises the importance of theoretical training and education as a guide to action.

We hope that reading *A House of Cards* will inspire you to join. Putting its proposals into practice is the big challenge of today. You can apply to join by sending an email to info@aworldtowin.net, filling in the form at www.aworldtowin.net, texting/phoning 07871 745258 or by post to AWTW, PO Box 942, London, SW1V 2AR.

We have an extensive website featuring:

▶ a daily blog, where you can comment on current developments
▶ news about campaigns for democratic rights and against low pay
▶ wide-ranging reportage of anti-slavery and self-determination movements today and yesterday including Palestine, Haiti, the Sahara region
▶ conference reports and podcasts
▶ book, film, art, theatre, music reviews
▶ ideas, philosophy and economic theory resources
▶ online purchasing of AWTW publications.

www.aworldtowin.net

Running a Temperature
an action plan for the eco-crisis

By Penny Cole and Philip Wade

First in **A World to Win**'s action guide series, *Running a Temperature* offers 64 pages of clearly presented research, analysis and an integrated approach for action. At a time when the first primate extinction in more than a century is imminent and many plant and animal species are disappearing due to hunting, habitat loss and climate change, half-measures are clearly no solution.

Running a Temperature shows how the capitalist economic and political elites have shown themselves to be part of the problem and a barrier to effective action to halt global warming and its catastrophic effect on the planet. Its action plan makes concrete proposals for re-organising energy, transport, the economy and food. Published in 2007 at £3.65 incl p&p.

That capitalism and climate change are inextricably linked is beyond doubt. *Running a Temperature* provides a clear and alternative framework for human existence beyond capitalism together with the best action plan to combat the dire predictions of climate change I have seen.

Dr Boris Kelly-Gerreyn
marine scientist

A World to Win

A rough guide to a future without global capitalism

analyses how corporate-driven globalisation shapes every aspect of modern society and uniquely suggests practical alternatives to the rule of transnational capitalism. The book:

- analyses the impact of profit-driven globalisation in a number of areas: alienation, economy, the state, culture, ecology and science
- puts forward a series of proposals which would revolutionise the economy, the state and our attitude towards culture and the Earth's ecosystems
- discusses human nature and our capacity to carry through change and puts forward a new concept for a political party.

This "rough guide" to a non-capitalist future is a manifesto which succeeds in combining polemic with some serious research. For example, their section on the state is unusually well-informed on issues such as the role of law and the rule of law.

Bill Bowring
Professor of Law, Birkbeck College, London University

At a time when political parties and nation states have become sub-systems of profit-driven globalisation, the world's future appears full of gloom and doom. *A World to Win* is a breath of fresh air – forceful, logical and absorbing to read.

Dr Ghayasuddin Siddiqui
Leader of the Muslim Parliament of Great Britain

This is a welcome addition to the growing literature prepared to argue that "There Is An Alternative". The book pulls no punches and its hard-hitting style will no doubt invite criticism. But this is exactly why it was written and deserves to be read.

Steve Fleetwood
Senior lecturer, the Department of Organisation, Work and Technology, Lancaster University

---

How to buy *A World to Win*

**online at www.aworldtowin.net or
by post (£11.99 incl. p&p) from
Lupus Books PO Box 942 London SW1V 2AR**

A rough guide to a future without global capitalism

A World to Win

Paul Feldman & Corinna Lotz